Praise for *Odyssey of Ashes*

"This compelling and heartw your heartstrings. The story death of the author's husb emanates from each page, for her suffering. This book wraps its arms around you and takes hold of your soul. I highly recommend this heartfelt and beautifully written book. *Odyssey of Ashes* is a must-read memoir."

—Dr. JOAN STEIDINGER, author of *Stand Up and Shout Out*

"Cheryl Krauter's gripping memoir traces her journey as she slowly heals from her husband's unexpected death. Her descriptions of his death itself and of her frantic, disoriented interactions with police and paramedics are raw and unforgettable. Her later encounters with helpers, such as a hungry hummingbird and a Montana fly fisherman named 'Dirty Mike,' are wry and poignant. Krauter's book pulses with sorrow and fierce aliveness as she grapples with the finality of death."

—KATHRYN RIDALL, PhD, author of *Dreaming at the Gates: How Dreams Guide Us*

"Though no one experiences the loss of a loved one in the same way, you need to add Krauter's *Odyssey of Ashes* to the shelf of great modern books on grief. Starting with the night of her husband's death—the suddenness, the casual care and callousness of those who responded—and ending with an evocation of Mexico's Day of the Dead, this memoir covers a lot of territory. Krauter is a cancer survivor herself, and the couple already knew to treat each day as if it were their last. Death puts that knowledge to the test, and this book is her testimony."

—SEAN ELDER, coauthor of *Great Is the Truth: Secrecy, Scandal and the Quest for Justice at the Horace Mann School*

"This is a tender and courageous love story of Cheryl Krauter's sacred journey through grief and the loss of her dear husband, John. Her lyrical writing flows like the rivers we travel on with her, touching the wild river of her soul. A story that does not end but reaches beyond into myth, ritual, and the archetype of sorrow and renewal of the wild woman inside her."

—BARBARA SAPIENZA, author of *Anchor Out* and *The Laundress*

"*Odyssey of Ashes* is a poignant, intimate journey through the grief of losing a loved one to recovery. Cheryl Krauter is not afraid to honestly share her struggles and triumphs. She draws the reader in as a fisherman reels in a catch, and having worked with Cheryl for several years, I expected nothing less."

—ANDREA KNOBLOCH, medical editor at *Oxford University Press*

"Written in an enjoyable, flowing format with chapters divided between two main sections, Krauter's book will break your heart. . . . I highly recommend this book for those who've lost a spouse and want to understand how one woman is working through it."

—SHAWN LATORRE, *StoryCircle Book Reviews*

ODYSSEY
of
ASHES

ODYSSEY

of

ASHES

A Memoir of
Love, Loss, and Letting Go

CHERYL KRAUTER

SHE WRITES PRESS

Published 2021
Printed in the United States of America
Print ISBN: 978-1-64742-132-8
E-ISBN: 978-1-64742-133-5
Library of Congress Control Number: 2021900674

For information, address:
She Writes Press
1569 Solano Ave #546
Berkeley, CA 94707

Interior design by Tabitha Lahr

She Writes Press is a division of SparkPoint Studio, LLC.

For John, always.

*"Sometimes I go about pitying myself.
And all the while I am being carried on
great winds across the sky."*
—OJIBWE SAYING

Part I

CHAPTER I

This is the day
you realize
how easily the thread
is broken
between this world
and the next . . .
—David Whyte

It's 3:30 a.m. My husband wakes up with back pain. Lying next to him in bed, barely conscious and groggy, I rub the spot; it feels tight, but after years of back problems, that's nothing unusual.

Unable to lie still, he gets up to go into the next room to stretch, and I anxiously trail behind and stand, hovering, like he always hates me to do.

"Can I do anything?"

"Get the foam roller; that might help."

I hurry into the bedroom, grab our large foam roller, and bring it to him. I stand over him, watching as he adjusts himself on it, trying to work through the pain in his back, hoping something will pop and release the suffering. Nothing seems to be helping, but my job is to reassure him.

He asks for some pain medication he was given, but never took, for a surgery earlier this year. He doesn't like pain meds, doesn't like how they make him feel; later, I will realize this is the moment I should have known how wrong things were, but for now I simply grab them from the medicine cabinet and hurriedly read the instructions. "You can take two."

No, he only wants one. *Well*, I think to myself, *maybe it's not too bad then.*

I'm watching, and I can see the stretching isn't helping. He's lying on top of the roller and moving slowly, taking different positions, trying to unlock the tension, his breath labored. My heart begins to pound as I watch him struggle. He doesn't usually spend this much time working with the roller. He doesn't spend this amount of time out of bed trying to deal with pain. Mostly, he doesn't let on how much pain he's experiencing.

There's a cold feeling in my body as I watch him struggle, but I force myself to stay optimistic. *We've been here before*, I remind myself. Again, later I'll understand that I should have known this time was different, but you only see these things in retrospect. The intensity of my own anxiety, how concerned I felt when he asked for drugs—these were clues that this time wasn't the same as other times before. I should have known.

I'm woozy and still hovering when he tells me to return to bed to get some sleep. He's always telling me to get some sleep. He's the only person who can say this to me without my finding it annoying. In fact, he's the only person I have ever known who can calm my restlessness. Ironic, considering his impatient nature. He'll be pissed off if I stay here, anxiously monitoring his every breath.

You're hovering, he must be thinking. It won't help if I stay and monitor him. It will only make him tense. Everything is already too uneasy, too uncomfortable. I can't help him. I'll upset him even more if I linger over him with my nervous watchfulness.

Stop it.

"Let me know if you need anything," I say.

"I love you," we tell each other. We've had an agreement since the time of my cancer that these should always be the last words we speak before parting, just in case it's the last contact we ever have. We say "I love you" to each other.

I leave him lying on the floor, stretching, and dutifully pad back to bed. He'll be okay. He's not clammy. He's not nauseous. He's not short of breath. *He'll be fine*, I tell myself.

But moments after I lie down, I suddenly feel panicky. I am clammy. I am nauseous. I am short of breath. Maybe we have food poisoning? What is happening?

As I attempt to get comfortable in bed, a terrible wind begins to howl all around me. It's a sound unlike any noise I've ever heard, reverberating from the other room. It's like the winds of a tornado ripping through our home. Then a procession of noises: a deeply guttural gasp for air, a roaring snort combined with the loudest snore I have ever heard. These horrifying sounds are accompanied by the sound of a rushing, watery release, a torrent of some kind of liquid. Is that a waterfall? Has the ceiling collapsed?

I levitate from the bed and run into the family room, where I find John sitting up on the couch in his usual place, a well-worn seat in front of the television he sits in so often that the cushions are molded to fit his body. It annoys the shit out of me how much time he spends there, actually, because I want him to be more active, get some exercise, move more. I can pretty much always count on finding him there for large parts of the day—a fact that is both aggravating and comforting.

A desolate quiet fills the space. It feels like the air's been sucked out of the room. I sit beside him, next to him. Is he asleep? *Don't wake him*, I think, *let him rest.* But then I worry. Has he passed out from the medication? Is that okay? In the darkness, I sit with him, and when I finally touch him . . .

He is too still. That's when I notice that he's peed all over himself, the rug. *Oh my God, he's not breathing.* I put my hand under his nose; there is no air coming out. He is not breathing in. I place my hand on his chest, his belly, and find no movement. *Oh no. Oh my God.* No breath, no sound . . . no response.

Before I know what I'm doing I am pleading for help on the phone to 911. How did I get to the phone? How did I dial 911?

"My husband is not breathing!" I shout at the woman on the line. "You have to send someone."

"Can you move him, ma'am?"

"No, I cannot move him."

"Is he breathing?"

"No, he is not breathing. What the fuck! Send the paramedics!" I yell to the inane, disembodied female voice on the other end of the line.

"Is he on hospice?"

"No. Please, please, they need to get here."

She keeps asking me if he is on hospice, whether I can move him, and whether he's on hospice, over and over again. No, I cannot move him, and no no no, he is not on hospice. She's actually annoyed with me. She needs to ask these questions, she says. I don't care what she needs, some stupid fucking protocol while time is passing or has stopped. I don't know which is real. And then I am shaking and screaming, "Get the fucking paramedics here now!"

When do the paramedics arrive? Do they get there in the requisite five minutes needed to save a life? Did they rush here? I don't know. I didn't hear any sirens.

A big man is at my door. He won't come in because he's afraid of my old, crippled dog. It all passes in a fog— the paramedic's arrival, his insistence that my dog, who can barely stand up without assistance, be shut in another room before they enter the house. *Five minutes is passing. Five minutes is surely over. Get to my husband!* This big man is afraid of my dog, who is nowhere near the room where John is and where all of this has transpired.

They're rushing through the house now, springing into action. There's a fireman. He is handsome, like most firemen. How bizarre to notice this right now.

"Sir, sir, can you hear me?" The paramedic asks John.

"Sir, can you hear me?"

The big man's enormous, chunky fingers are on John's neck, and then his face freezes. Suddenly, John is on the floor. They are ripping off his T-shirt, leaving him naked. There are instruments scattered all around him. I see them bring out a defibrillator; they're attaching those adhesive defibrillator pads to his chest, trying to make an electrical current pass through to his heart, trying to get a pulse, trying to find a breath. *Set. Set. Set.* They're trying to get an electrical current into him, trying to restart his heart. They're placing a plastic tube down his throat . . . intubating him.

"Clear. Clear."

Men are scrambling around John. I stare wildly at the scene before me. I should go to the next room, the big man says. I am frozen in horror. I cannot move.

Suddenly, I'm in the kitchen. How did I get here? Where is my dog? A woman is with me. She is young, quiet, but she seems kind. Her eyes are big and dark; she wears a hijab. What is it like for her to see a man lying naked on the floor? Why am I thinking this during this trauma?

She is saying something to me: "Are you all right?"

"No, no, I am not all right."

The big man comes into the kitchen and looms over me. "I need to prepare you. We cannot find a pulse." With that, he turns and strides in his heavy boots back to what is quickly becoming a death chamber in my family room.

I cannot stop shaking; my entire body rolls with spasms. My teeth are rattling against one another. The woman looks sympathetic, but she doesn't speak. I am shaking and gasping for air. She is silent. There is horrible absence of breath all around me. I feel carried along by a wind that is spewing from the mouth of a devil.

Oh no, the big man is coming back down the hall. It's too soon; he should not be leaving his post with John. His boots pound the floor. I feel an earthquake coming. *No! No! Go back to John. Don't come here. Go away; you're not welcome here.* He is standing over me. He is telling me that my husband is dead. There's nothing they could have done. It happened in less than five minutes.

I should have known. I should have known. The connection between John and me is strongly woven, our bond a somatic attachment. I know him too well not to have known. Not to have trusted my instincts. But could I have saved him? Surely, I could have saved him.

I run to the family room. The other paramedics are still here. I fall to the floor and hold John. I hear wailing from some distant place, a guttural cry I do not recognize as my own voice. *No. Oh God. No.*

I'm sitting at my dining room table. How did I get here? The handsome fireman is talking to me, asking me questions. I'm lost in a foreign land, and I do not speak the language. I cannot read the signs. Someone says something about an autopsy.

"Do you want an autopsy?"

"What?"

"It really isn't necessary; there's been no crime."

"What?" What is he asking me? "No, no autopsy. Why?"

Then I'm signing something. How many times have we all heard that we should always read a document before we sign it? But I cannot see the writing on the form. I don't know what I'm signing. It must be a document of death. There is no warranty involved. The fireman is kind and protects me from the big paramedic, who is asking me things I cannot hear. Where is the woman? Has she silently floated away? When did they all leave?

A young policeman is here. When did he arrive? He is caring and concerned. He asks me who can come to be with me. I don't know. I can't say. I don't know who can come. Who will come to be with me? What am I going to do? I run back to the family room and get back onto the floor with John. I'm a madwoman on the ground. When I put my arms around him, I discover some adhesive patches the paramedics used to attempt to shock him back into life still stuck to his chest. I carefully pull them off, not wanting to hurt him.

Clutching John, I feel him flying out of his body like a comet hurtling through space. My breath is taken away as I experience his departure as a strong gust of wind that knocks me back onto the floor next to him. He's carried away from me, from this world, to another place of consciousness, a land I cannot travel to . . . not yet.

We have talked about death as a spiritual transition for years, sharing our beliefs and reflections, but the conversation had taken on a serious sense of reality when I was diagnosed with cancer in 2007. We used to take bets on who would go first. On paper, it looked like I was the likely candidate, but he believed it would be him. I guess in the end he won that bet. We sometimes wondered about how we would each die. He always said, "Oh, I'll probably just explode someday." This prediction was informed and fueled by his profound impatience, his quick temper, and his absolute inability to suffer fools gladly (and certainly not silently). After his pronouncement, we would laugh.

On this dark morning, it's no longer funny.

I ask him to tell me what it's like, this journey we've spoken of so often. And I begin to accept that we will not share this voyage, this crossing. He is migrating to another time and space, and I am being left behind. This cannot be happening, but it is.

Looking up, I see the young policeman. He stays close by. He does not leave me. Brendon, his name is Brendon. He is talking to me. Telling me that this is a wonderful house, that he can tell there is much love in this house, this home. He keeps connecting with me, helping me figure out who to call. Finally, I call a neighbor. She doesn't pick up. Well, it's 4:00 a.m. People turn off their cell phones at night. I call John's sister. Her phone number does not work. I dial again and again. Nothing works; no one is there. I call his niece. She is there, immediately concerned by the fact of my calling at 4:00 a.m.

"John is dead," I tell her.

"What, what, no," she says. "Oh no," she says, and she begins to cry.

"I cannot reach your mom; her phone doesn't work."

She says, "I'll reach her," and somehow she does.

John's sister calls.

"He's dead," I say. "John's dead."

"Oh no, oh no," she says. "We'll be there as soon as possible."

Brendon stands by. He will not leave me alone.

Someone calls the mortuary. They won't come until I say it's time. How is it possible that it will ever feel like the "right time"? Who called them? Was it the handsome fireman? Did he do it before he left?

John's sister and her husband arrive. We sit in my living room in shock. We are talking, but I don't know what we are talking about. I go back to John. Cathy follows me into the family room to see her brother. She stands and looks at him.

"Cover his little legs," she says as she looks down at her younger brother, her little brother. John was small, a little boy who didn't grow until he was in high school. Cathy, the older sister, had friends who thought he was cute and would respond to him with hugs. I remember him telling me about one well-endowed girl who used to hug him tightly to her, his face pressed against her breasts; he told me that he never once objected or turned away.

Does he feel cold? Does he feel anything, wherever he is now? Where is he now?

She stays, looking at her younger brother. She's been the one who's struggled with so much illness, and now she's the only person left of her family of origin.

Before I know what I'm doing, I'm on the floor. I am stroking his forehead. I put my arms around him, holding his stillness to me. His face is peaceful, and I hate hate hate the stupid cliché—"he looks at peace"—for being a reality in this moment. Fiercely, I hope that he really is peaceful, that this sudden exit from the life he has known is tranquil.

I ask him to tell me what this passage is like, but he is silent. He will not be able to tell me about his journey. He will never talk to me again.

I cannot believe that he has left me. He has also left our son behind. I have to call him in Los Angeles, where he's in school. I have to ready myself for this call, but, not surprisingly, it goes to voicemail. I text, thinking that may be received or viewed before a phone call. I am stoic, preparing to give him this shock while he is miles away from home.

Minutes later, how many, I don't know, he calls. "What's up?" I hear caution in his voice, the edge of fear in the background. Of course he knows something must be dreadfully wrong and that a call or text at five in the morning is nothing casual—no funny emoji, no "hey, just thinking of you."

Dad is dead.

What?

What?!

What happened?!

I tell him. I cannot believe it either.

Your father is dead.

The sun begins to rise.

I remain with John. "Would it be okay if he stayed home with me just a little longer?" I ask Brendon. In a little while, he will leave our home—the home he loved, the home Brendon, the policeman, says is such a wonderful home—for the last time. "Just a few more moments, please."

Who called the mortuary to say it's time to come? It must have been me. Two more men come into the house, but they're not rushing; they come quietly with a gurney, and they wait for me to tell them when they can take the body away. John has become a body. I have to let go.

"I have to let you go," I tell him. "I know I do. I promise I will not hold you to this earth. I have to let you go."

In my heart, I know that John's spirit has left. I also know that it will never be the right time, that this will not get easier. I have a crazy thought of the mortuary men helping me get him back into bed. It is that thought that makes me realize it's time. I turn to the mortuary men. "It's time," I say.

Like the paramedics, they tell me it's better for me not to watch this process. I'm touched and grateful for their respect. And then they are rolling a gurney with a black body bag out of our house, out of what is now my house. They are leaving with my husband. He is leaving me.

Goodbye.

I promise I will not hold on.

Goodbye.

I promise I will let you go.

CHAPTER 2

The last words my husband and I ever spoke to each other were "I love you."

CHAPTER 3

Aging, sickness, and death are suffering.
Loss, grief, and despair are suffering.
To lose what you love is suffering.
—BUDDHA

"You can't go alone," Diane says after she asks what will happen the day after John dies and I respond by telling her I'm going to sign papers at the mortuary.

"I'll be okay," I mumble over the phone.

"I'm coming," she says firmly.

"Okay." This reply comes from somewhere amid my wildness and numbness. How can I feel so much and nothing at the same time? What is this reality I am living in? I have no idea.

The next morning, we're walking through the massive front doors of the mortuary. They're so heavy that we have to struggle to open them, to enter the unearthly quietness of the lobby. They certainly make it tough to get into a place no one wants to enter to begin with. The people inside are all dressed in black suits; they seem friendly enough. It's cold in here. Why do they keep the temperature this low for the living? Will we, like the dead, rot if we're left out too long in the warm air?

Hello, they say. What is your name, they ask. Oh, yes. Oh, yes, we are expecting you.

I keep expecting the Grim Reaper to round the corner.

Please have a seat. Please wait here.

Please . . . please . . . make this not be real, I think. *Please . . .*

A blond woman greets us, and we move into an austere office. She is sorry. We are sorry. I, most of all, am sorry. If John were here, I imagine, he would say, "If it's one thing you are, it's sorry."

Greeted by more papers, I find myself for the second time in twenty-four hours signing things that I cannot manage to read or understand. I don't care what I am scribbling my signature on. I go through the motions of knowing what I am doing, pretending I understand what is expected, as I now face the business of death—the contracts, the fees, learning the cost of his obituary, deciding about whether to include a photo for the newspaper (which nearly doubles the price of the few words that will describe him and the life he has just exited).

In spiritually oriented cultures, the care of the dead is personal and meaningful. Rituals for blessing the dying as they move on and comforting the living who are left behind in the wake of their departure are practiced. But I do not live on a remote Tibetan mountain, nor am I in a small village beside the Ganges River in India where this perspective on dying exists. I am in a small room in an icy building in the United States full of dead people lying in large freezer containers awaiting burial or cremation. As a spiritual person living in the material, urban world, I worry that I am not sending John off with grace. There is no presence of the sacred in this gray, cavernous building.

"No, I don't want a coffin," I say. "He wanted cremation, and I will take his ashes." I will take John's ashes to a trout stream, to a mighty river, which was his request. He wanted what was remaining of his physical body scattered where he might cast his line into the water for eternity—or at least keep watch on the water for the errant trout he loved to trick.

But today, I must write checks, sign papers, order death certificates. Dully and dutifully, I do what is expected. I feel nothing.

"Do you want to watch the cremation?" the blond lady asks. "Actually, we don't recommend it."

"You shouldn't look," said the paramedic who tried to save John's life.

"It's better if you don't look," said the mortuary men taking John's body.

"We don't recommend that you look," says the blond woman now.

No one says, "You should look at him, look at his face, his hands, touch his chest. Look as long as you need to, because his soul is leaving this body forever. You will never get another chance to look. You should look and, in that way, honor him."

I feel a sudden, intense need to look at John. "I would like to look at him now," I tell the blond woman. "Do not cremate him until our son comes." Our son needs to look, to see his father for the last time, to make it real that he is, indeed, dead and to understand that this is not just a nightmare, that death is real. As a twenty-three-year-old who's lost his father at the pivotal moment when he's facing the first real challenges of adulthood, he needs closure. It's important that he be a part of these final moments of his father's life. It matters that this life-changing event be real. In our so-called sophisticated culture, we barely recognize death, let alone honor it. We "don't recommend" witnessing it . . .

"Yes, we can do that. There is barely enough time for your son to get here, but we can hold the body for a couple more days."

What is this woman's name? I wonder for a fleeting second. But it doesn't matter.

Someone must continue to look, to not turn away, to look upon John's face before he's taken away forever.

"I would like to see him now," I say again.

"We'll get him ready for viewing," she says.

For viewing . . . He's become an art piece, a photograph, a newly decorated room, an antiquity.

Then Diane and I are being led down a dim hallway. As we pass the receptionist at the front desk, we notice that she's playing a game of solitaire on her computer. Diane and I look at each other and almost break into a fit of laughter at this bizarre sight. *How is the game going?* I wonder. *Is she winning?* As I prepare to look at my dearly departed husband, I'm not meditating in a cave high up in the mountains in Tibet, praying, or preparing his body for cremation; I am not on the Ganges River building a funeral pyre for him. Instead, as I walk down a corridor to the room where he waits for me, as I make this long, breathless walk to my husband's body, I'm passing a woman who is playing computer solitaire. This stark hallway is devoid of anything remotely passing for sacred.

We enter a large room with chairs set up along the walls. They're ready for a crowd, but only two of us are present—three if you count the casket where John is lying, eyes closed, still, so still. I bend over him and sob convulsively, gasping for air, as a cold wind chills the room. His face is icy, but I cannot stop touching it, smoothing his hair, kissing him. I am crying so hard I might throw up. Diane sits quietly, holding the scene; she doesn't intrude with attempts at comforting me. She is there.

At some point, I turn to her and signal we can leave.

"Would you like to sit for a moment?" she asks.

"Yes, yes, I would," I gasp.

We sit next to each other, looking ahead at John's body. Then, closing our eyes, we begin to meditate. Both of us practice Buddhist meditation. Now, together, we sit in honor of the dead and in sorrow and suffering for the living.

The quiet surrounds us in the freezing funereal tomb.

Diane begins to offer the words used to honor the dead, to help John on his journey. I sit silently, weeping . . . weeping . . . breathing . . . breathing . . .

In Buddhism, they say, "The soul rises to the nine heavens; the spirit falls to the nine abysses. The living suffers in grief; the dead settle in peace." On this unimaginably dark Sunday morning in May, we sit and honor the journey of my husband's soul with one of my favorite Buddhist meditations:

May you be filled with loving kindness.
May you be well on your journey.
May you be safe from whatever dangers befall you.
May your passage be filled with light.
May you be happy.
May you find peace.
May you be free from suffering.

Before we leave, we bow.

CHAPTER 4

Many go fishing all their lives without
knowing that it is not fish they are after.
—Henry David Thoreau

The first time John and I went fishing, it was nearly our last.

It was 1987, and I stood in the middle of a pristine trout stream in Northern California, barely able to move in the ridiculous getup known in the fly-fishing world as waders. Getting that suit on was like rolling a pair of rubber panty-hose up the lower half of my body. I resembled a large hot dog. I was laced into heavy boots *also* known as waders, and it was becoming clear to me that wading through currents and over rocks that appeared to have been marinated in olive oil, while dressed in a sauna suit accessorized by "wading boots," was an acquired skill. I was carrying a rod—not a pole, a rod—and I was wildly flinging it around in hopes of releasing the line remotely far enough out so that I might be able to catch a wild trout on the fly, only to then release it back into the wild from whence it swam.

Attempting not to stumble on the slippery stones and fall into the lightly rushing current, I continued to make nest-like piles of fishing line that John had to continually untangle. After a few hours of fishing, my line was mucky from the vegetation in the stream and I'd caught quite a few large boulders, each of which I excitedly assumed to be gargantuan trout until John pointed out that my line wasn't moving, the stasis indicating that there was no fish involved. I had also managed to snag a number of the tree branches overhanging the stream—already, I was somewhat of an expert at catching "tree trout."

John was practically standing on top of me, yelling instructions and constantly telling me everything I was doing wrong, which was, actually, pretty much *everything*. At some point, his legendary impatience emerged, then exploded, and he stormed down the river, leaving me wobbling about in my waders and wading boots in furious tears. Really? I'd never done this before and I was already expected to know what I was doing?

We'd been dating for about six months and had found many things to connect over in that time; so far, it had all been exciting, fun, and passionate. I'd agreed to this fishing adventure out of a desire to join John in his lifelong love of fly-fishing. But in this moment, not only was I not at all sure about this guy; I also wasn't all that enamored with the illustrious sport of fly-fishing. What the hell was all the fuss about?

Then again, we were at a stunningly beautiful river in the foothills of Northern California on a brilliant fall day, and I was quite taken with standing in the middle of a stream in the arms of nature . . .

Thus began my fly-fishing adventures.

Fly-fishing, as defined by Merriam-Webster, is "a method of fishing in which an artificial fly is cast by use of a fly rod, a reel, and a relatively heavy oiled or treated line." The first known use of this word comes from 1653 and describes an angling method in which an artificial "fly" is used to catch fish. The fly is cast using a fly rod, reel, and specialized weighted line. Casting a nearly weightless fly, or lure, requires casting techniques significantly different from other forms of casting. How hard could that be?

Well, let me tell you, it's plenty hard, and I was in a relationship with a man who was a master at it and who desperately wanted me to fish with him.

The things we do for love.

John was twelve years old when he caught his first fish on a fly in Cisco Grove, a blip of a town that sits along the highway leading to Lake Tahoe in California. Whenever we drove this stretch of highway, I would comment on my search for the California Historical Landmark plaque marking the spot of this auspicious event: *Cisco Grove: Site of John Leonard Catching His First Fish on a Fly, circa 1958.* He invented a contraption that served as a rod, tied a make-shift fly, and somehow attached the two. After that, he was hooked, just like a fish, for the rest of his life.

Along the winding road that passes by the Eel River in the foothills of Northern California, there should be another historical plaque honoring the survival of the pioneering days of our relationship: *Site of First Fishing Trip of Cheryl Krauter and John Leonard: Both Survived and the Relationship Bloomed, circa 1987.*

CHAPTER 5

Casting for Recovery was founded on the principles that the natural world is a healing force and that women with breast cancer deserve one weekend—free of charge and free of the stresses from medical treatment, home, or workplace—to experience something new and challenging in a beautiful, safe environment. The mission of Casting for Recovery® (CfR) is to enhance the quality of life of women with breast cancer through a unique retreat program that combines breast cancer education and peer support with the therapeutic sport of fly fishing. The program offers opportunities for women to find inspiration, discover renewed energy for life and experience healing connections with other women and nature. CfR serves women of all ages, in all stages of breast cancer treatment and recovery, at no cost to participants.

—FROM THE CASTING FOR RECOVERY WEBSITE

My name was drawn!

In 2008, eight years before he died, John told me about a nonprofit group called Casting for Recovery that gifted retreats to women with breast cancer, offering them a chance to meet one another, spend restful and restorative time away from their busy lives . . . and learn about fly-fishing. A group of experienced women fly-fishers had discovered that the action of casting a fly rod actually soothed the physical wounds of breast cancer and helped heal lymphedema, a painful swelling that happens when the body's lymphatic fluid is unable to circulate properly and builds up in the soft tissues. People with cancer who have undergone lymph node removal and/or radiation as part of their treatment are at risk for developing this condition, and it is a particular threat to women with breast cancer.

CfR also recognized the emotional and psychic wounds of a breast cancer diagnosis by offering nurturing support groups for survivors and giving them a moment in time when someone else would cook, do the dishes, and make the bed for them.

John was excited when he found out about CfR because I'd been diagnosed with rare and aggressive metastatic triple negative breast cancer in 2007 and had endured a grueling treatment that involved surgery, chemotherapy, and radiation. I'd lost nearly thirty pounds and *every* hair on my body. I'd suffered radiation burns, mouth ulcers, and thrush, and at one point my eyes had turned bright red, a color that matched the chemo medicine pouring through my veins.

The chance to attend a CfR workshop involved me entering my name in a drawing with the hope of winning the grand prize of a ticket to a fall retreat on the Pit River at Clearwater Lodge in Northern California.

Luck was with me, and I was one of the women randomly picked to attend. I was not yet a year out of treatment for breast cancer at that point and was still pretty wobbly on my feet because of severe peripheral neuropathy. The brutal chemotherapy treatment I'd undergone had saved my life, but it had also left my body in shreds. Barely able to feel the pedals of my car but undaunted, I drove north on a crisp, golden fall day to join up with the other "one in eight women" who'd also been dealt the bad hand of a breast cancer diagnosis.

We spent the weekend talking with one another, learning the skills of fly-fishing, and eating healthy food lovingly prepared in a gorgeous setting. A fly-fisher named Peg was the coordinator. She was an energetic woman whose caring flowed out over the group in massive waves. We were scheduled to fish on the morning of the last day, when we'd meet our River Helpers, experienced fly-fishers who donated their time to guiding participants in the fly-fishing section of the retreat. We each got our own River Helper; I was paired with an older, kind man who himself was a cancer survivor.

That day, I was unable to stay for long in the river, as the cold water, even through my waders, created such a deep ache in my legs that I had trouble feeling my feet. The pain was so intense, in fact, that I had difficulty wading out of the river and could not stand up once I was on the shore. I was still so sick from cancer treatment, and my guide held on to me as I struggled. I spent the rest of the morning sitting in a camp chair, hoping the pain would subside enough for me to walk back to the vans waiting to take us back from the river to the lodge. Staring out at the river before me, I listened to my River Helper tell his own cancer story.

When I returned from the weekend, I told John about the River Helpers and how CfR was looking for volunteers. Without hesitation, he applied. He went on to spend the next eight years guiding women on these river retreats, women who told him their stories as he imparted his extensive knowledge about casting techniques. At times, when it felt right, he also shared his own story—the fears and feelings he had about me having cancer.

Each time John returned from these trips, he would share his river experiences with me. Sometimes I felt like I had been there right beside him in whatever river he had been fishing. He and Peg developed a wonderful connection that continued when she moved to Montana several years later so she could live close to some mighty rivers where all fly-fishers yearn to fish. John's time with CfR was extremely meaningful to him, as it gave him a chance to give back to those struggling with a diagnosis of breast cancer. Yes, he got to get away and fish too (and, indeed, he always took a few fishin' days for himself when he went), but it was the retreats that meant the most to him. Being a River Helper gave him a chance to heal from all he had gone through when I had breast cancer, when he felt so frightened and helpless in the face of a disease he couldn't fix. His involvement gave him a place to give back, a way to feel a sense of power after witnessing a devastating illness that can spiral out of control at any moment.

CfR holds an annual gala that includes a raffle for a fly-fishing float trip on some of the most coveted rivers in North America. Floating down a magnificent river in a small boat with an experienced local guide who knows and understands a river like the back of his or her hand is the dream of every serious fly-fisher. Spending half a day in some remote location with the promise of meeting an ancient trout does not come easy or cheap, and in modern times, this activity has become the territory of the wealthy. John had a bucket list that included fishing the most coveted of the world's great streams, creeks, and rivers. The CfR prize offered the hope of crossing one off of his list, and each year John bought a fifty-dollar ticket.

CHAPTER 6

When much is taken, something is returned.
—TERRY PRATCHETT

In October 2016, I return to a river in Northern California where John and I fished together for many years. It is said that you never step into the same river twice, but I think that maybe each time we wade into a river, we return to some primal beginning, the currents flowing around us and changing as each moment passes. Like the years of a long relationship taken suddenly by a devastating current of disappearance, what was present becomes memory.

We had a tradition of spending time at Lake Tahoe, California—first as a couple and then, after our son was born, as a family. These trips always involved some time spent fishing. Sometimes we'd stay at the cabin of a friend and fellow fly fisherman, sometimes in one of the lakeside resorts. We'd spend at least a week; when time and money permitted, we'd stay for two. Those vacation spots had to be reserved a year in advance, and this year, John and I had been looking forward to the weeklong October break we carved out. We were to spend it with another couple—dear friends of ours, Bill and Shash.

Bill and I met when he was two and I was three. Our families lived in an apartment complex on Lake Washington on an island just across from Seattle, and we became committed little partners in crime while our parents drank and played bridge. This was an era when children enjoyed more freedom to roam, getting into all kinds of trouble that no one ever suspected. Billy was the thin, wiry one and I was the bossy, chunky one. In one black-and-white photograph I love from this period, Billy—a rare serious expression on his face—is dressed in my pink tutu and is holding his spindly little stick arms akimbo in a perfect ballet position. In another shot, I'm wearing a red candy-striped nightie, sick and unable to come out to play. My lips are pressed against the glass door, and Billy is standing on the other side, kissing me back through the glass as he stands outside in his miniature hunter's flap hat.

Billy and I remained close buddies until my family moved to California in the 1960s, but we lost contact after working together at a lodge on the Olympic Peninsula in Washington in 1969, when he was seventeen and I was eighteen. I fled back to California after a month in a drugged-up and messy scene that ended in tragedy when a kid, believing he could fly, fell to his death from the top of a water tower. That was the last time Billy and I saw each other for many years. At some point in the 1980s, my mother told me that Bill had become an investment banker in New York City, but I steadfastly refused to believe that the wild hippie child I remembered was wearing a three-piece suit and working in a bank.

In 2009, John and I went to Seattle to attend the wedding of a friend, and I became obsessed with finding Bill. I'd heard he'd moved back to the Pacific Northwest, forsaking his life as an investment banker. A cancer diagnosis can swallow you whole and spit you back out with the realization that you are not immortal and you'd better make the most of whatever time is left to you. "Time's a-wasting," my mother used to say when I would dawdle, and now I felt that urgency; I needed to find Billy. That wasn't too hard with the help of the Internet, and we agreed to meet at Pike Place Market in Seattle.

It had been forty years. I was slightly anxious about our meeting, and I wondered what seeing him again would be like. My Internet search had shown his support for Barack Obama, so I figured we couldn't have gone too far in different directions.

John and I were sitting at an outside café, drinking coffee, when Bill came into view. He and I looked at each other and immediately began to laugh hysterically. We flew back in time, and those two silly children we had never lost within ourselves sprang back to life.

Growing up in the Pacific Northwest means being born into the world of the salmon. As children, we ate planked salmon barbecued by our fathers long before it became an item on the menus of upscale restaurants. As I've gotten older and mortality has slapped me around a bit, I've felt like those salmon, thrashing their way back upstream to the place where they originated. I have watched salmon hurl themselves toward the home they somehow always know how to find, and it's amazed me every time. I wonder if my upbringing in the Pacific Northwest makes the pull of the spawning salmon, that desire for a return home, even more powerful.

It was on this trip that I met Bill's wife, Shash—an intelligent, sensitive, powerful woman deeply committed to social justice, education, and family—for the first time. To my great relief, I liked her at once.

Over the next seven years, Bill and Shash became dear friends of ours. Bill shared John's love of fly-fishing, and they joined forces on different streams and rivers. So when John died five months before the trip we'd planned with Bill and Shash, I was scared that it would be too painful to go without John. In my heightened vulnerability, I was also worried that Bill and Shash might not want to go with me when I was still so raw with grief. In the end, I decided to keep the reservation, and I was relieved and touched when Bill told me they were glad I'd decided to do so and were looking forward to spending time with me in Tahoe.

Four people have become three.

I drive up alone, and I will spend a few days by myself until my friends arrive. I am doing okay on the way, until I pass by the infamous Cisco Grove spot. I guess I am still okay after that, because I keep driving—though I probably should pull over until I stop sobbing.

I have brought John's ashes in the little carrying case from Sunset View Mortuary. I can't bear to go to Tahoe without him, so he sits in the passenger seat beside me in his small, but rather heavy, box on the way up.

Upon arriving at the same spot we were all together in a year ago, I haul everything up the stairs. As I struggle with a case of wine, I notice some men standing by the nearby barbecue; they clearly see me floundering but do nothing to help me. *Well*, I think to myself, *this is how it is now. Thirty years ago, those guys would have been falling all over themselves to help me. Last year, John carted the heavy stuff up the stairs.*

Now my goddamn husband is dead and I'm lugging the freakin' wine up the stairs alone, one step at a time.

I'm glad when my friends arrive. The next day, during a light snowfall, we decide to hike a familiar trail as the soft, silent snowflakes fall and glisten on evergreen branches, the wind gently scattering their whiteness around us. The three of us trudge across the crunchy ground in silence. On the path, a rare remaining fall leaf startles our vision with reds and browns. When it stops snowing, sunlight shines on the branches of the towering, ancient trees arching above us. The freshness of the cold mountain air fills our lungs, and the wind stings and reddens our cheeks.

We're hiking through the sparkling, shimmering, white, wintry world to get back to the car when the infernal ring of my cell phone disrupts our peaceful day. Annoyed by something that is completely within my control (after all, I not only brought the phone but also neglected to turn off the sound), I ignore it until we get back to the car.

After I'm seated in the car, I open my voice mail to the voice of John's fellow fly-fishing aficionado, Peg.

"Hello, Cheryl, it's Peg Miskin," she says. "I hope you're hanging in, and I have some news for you. The Casting for Recovery Gala was last night, and at the last minute I decided to include John's ticket in the raffle and threw it into the hopper with all of the other entries." She pauses. "Cheryl . . . I drew his name. John won the float trip. I fell apart and was too overcome to read it out loud; I had to hand it to someone else to announce."

She wants to offer me the trip, she says, to give me a chance to go and fulfill John's dream.

John purchased that ticket just a month prior to his death this spring, and now, after so many years of disappointing losses, he has finally won a prize that was on his bucket list: a guided fly-fishing float trip for two down the Madison River in Montana. The Madison River, known as a mecca for fly-fishing, is one of the great rivers of the world and runs through the epicenter of what many think of as the best fly-fishing region on the planet.

As I sob in the car, I marvel at the cruel joke the Genie of the Bucket List has played. From the back seat, Shash places her gentle, cool hands on my shoulders and silently holds me as I shudder. Thoughts and feelings pour out of me as I wail, "He wanted this so badly, and he'll never get to go. This was his trip, and now he finally won and it's too late. How can this happen?"

Bill, sitting in the driver's seat next to me, says quietly but firmly, "He got to fish a lot of rivers that he wanted to fish. He'd want you to go."

But this isn't on *my* bucket list. And yet maybe, in some unknown way, it was meant to be my trip all along. As sometimes happens, like when I was diagnosed with cancer, it's not the journey I would have chosen. Yet these are the cards that have been laid before me, and I know I will play the hand I've been dealt.

Is it a kind of madness to live out the dream of another? This question will plague me as the future I anticipated disintegrates into ash and I find myself contemplating bringing John to Montana in a small, plastic bag to one of the great rivers of his desires, fulfilling a wish on a bucket list that does not belong to me.

CHAPTER 7

> *"If we take eternity to mean not infinite temporal duration, but timelessness, then eternal life belongs to those who live in the present."*
> —LUDWIG WITTGENSTEIN

After John dies I am haunted by two recurrent images. In one, I'm in the middle of a large body of water with no land in sight—floating, treading water, and sometimes swimming in directionless motion. In the other, I am floating out in space, unattached and alone in an ink-black universe lit only by unrecognizable stars and strangely colored planets. I feel lost in a timeless space in the middle of the sea.

Albert Einstein's theory of relativity postulates that time is an illusion—a relative "fourth dimension" that slows down or speeds up depending on how fast you move relative to something else. My grief is timeless and has no known destination—past, present, and future have all become one. I wander the Milky Way and roll on large swells in the middle of the sea. I exist in a parallel reality beyond the known universe. All the while I commute to work, cook dinner, and pay bills. I stay afloat. I learn to breathe in airless space. I've become a time traveler.

As a child, one of my favorite movies was *The Time Machine*, an old black-and-white portrayal of the novel by H. G. Wells. On early Saturday mornings while my parents still slept, I watched it dozens of times, fascinated, lost in my own imaginary world. When I was a kid, my friends and I would ask one another what we would wish for if we had only one wish. My constant request was for a time machine. All my life I have dreamt of having one of my own. Now it seems I have one of my own making, as I become an explorer in this infinite stream of memory and loss.

CHAPTER 8

Fly-fishing is the contemplative man's recreation.
—Izaak Walton

"I need to go fishing to get whole," John would say before he'd head off to a stream or creek to do some fishing. As I became acquainted with the world of the angler, I came to understand that it's a kind of religion for those who embrace the sport, the art, of fly-fishing. The solace and quietude that standing in a river brings is profound, and I grew to deeply understand the need for the return to watery places. Being in a river brought me a tranquility I had never known, and it was this aspect of fly-fishing that helped me understand my husband's obsession. I would stand, gazing around at the birds, feeling the sun on my face, and listening to the soft rustle of the branches along the river, lost in time, and at some point, the guide who'd been hired to help me would inevitably remind me, "We're here to fish, Cheryl." *Oh* . . .

This obsession with fishing goes far back into history, all the way to the times of the Romans. Though the exact origin is unknown, it's believed that the first records of fly-fishing date back to second-century Rome, specifically to the Roman Claudius Aelianus, who gave a detailed description of how Macedonian anglers caught fish. I've not read this description, but with my considerable experience listening to fly-fishers discuss their craft, I have absolutely no doubt that it is excruciatingly detailed. Izaak Walton's *The Compleat Angler*, published in 1653 and one of the earliest "fishing bibles," helped popularize fly-fishing as a sport. When Walton describes the flies used in fly-fishing, he explains how, when he uses wool feathers, "the fish, attracted and maddened by the color, comes straight at it, thinking from the pretty sight to gain a dainty mouthful; when, however, it opens its jaws, it is caught by the hook, and enjoys a bitter repast, a captive."

Many fishing flies are gorgeous replicas of the actual bug they are meant to portray, and most accomplished fly-fishers tie most of their own flies. Some even invent new flies based on their knowledge and expertise of the waters they fish. After a day of fishing, John would sit and tie flies for the next day's outing. He had the eye and skill of an artist, and he produced some wonderful little critters. Regardless of the type of fly or the person tying it, the intention is always the same: entice the fish with what looks like a tasty morsel.

Fly-fishing has continued to evolve since its believed origin in Rome, and it's generally agreed upon that the modern fly-fishing of today would not exist without the development of the sport in the United Kingdom, Japan, and the United States. Writers, mostly male, have written volumes (once again making clear the obsession with all that fly-fishing represents, which is so much more than

throwing a line with an enticing "mouthful" for a fish)—
famous tales of fishing and the symbolism surrounding
it, stories of life, loss, redemption, and glory. Perhaps the
most famous is Norman Maclean's *A River Runs Through It*,
which was made into a film known in the fly-fishing world
as "The Movie." It was after the release of this movie in
1992 that the sport became the passion of every wannabe
fly fisherman hoping to emulate Brad Pitt casting enormous loops and rolls in the rivers of Montana.

After that, the sport exploded into a new popularity,
and the scene became more elite, which was not all that
bad for fishing guides scratching out a living in some of the
most magnificent spots in the world, the rivers of Montana
being one of those prime locations. But it was not so great
for the fishermen who'd been around long before the insur-
gence of those who, outfitted in expensive garb and excited
to report back from the famous places they had just gone
fly-fishing, were more interested in the status of the sport
than the spirit of it. Pristine locations became overcrowded,
and many inexperienced fishermen, believing themselves to
be experts, had no idea of stream etiquette—nor did they
appear to have much interest in learning how to behave on
a river. Fly-fishers are a territorial bunch, and I've witnessed
countless subtle, and not so subtle, conflicts over fishing
spots. Fly-fishing does pride itself on being a "gentleman's
sport," bringing to mind images of men in tweeds fishing
meandering streams in the United Kingdom. While the
American West is a rugged, expansive, and wild contrast
to Britain's small creeks and Japan's impeccable locales,
no matter where you go, there are still many spoken and
unspoken rules of etiquette in fly-fishing. But when the
entitled came to fish, the rules seemed not to apply.

John always hired a fishing guide when he went to a new river. The guide would show him the spots to fish, the type of equipment he would need, and, of course, the very vital information of which fly to use in those waters. As an experienced and masterful fly fisherman, he needed little help and instruction: just the directions to the best hole and what to dangle on the hook.

When I began coming along, however, we needed a guide to rescue me from tangled lines and hooks caught in trees and rocks. John and I had long ago learned that he was not the best guide or instructor for me, so to save our relationship he would also make sure to ferret out guides he thought might work well with me—basically good-humored, patient teachers who would babysit me during a day of fishing.

As my education in fly-fishing progressed, I was instructed on methods to bushwhack through tangled brambles while carefully carrying my rod so as not to snap it even before I got to the river. I learned to stand at the top of a cliff and look down at the water below me to see where a crafty fish might be lying. I was taught to be quiet and walk softly on the earth during my approach to the stream. (I have actually crawled on my knees toward a creek with no surrounding foliage, rod pointing straight ahead in one hand, in order to hide my murderous shadow from the fish resting beneath the water.)

One of the great characters in the fly-fishing world, Sheridan Anderson, published a small book called *The Curtis Creek Manifesto: A Guide to the Strategy, Finesse, Tactics, and Paraphernalia of Fly Fishing* in 1978. It has since sold over a million copies. In it, he writes that when fly-fishing is done right, "the water becomes a glorious shimmering three-dimensional chessboard" and the contest is "a game to be mastered thru skill, diligence and imagination." John gave me this book and also taught me to think like a fish, imagining where I might be resting in the water, the places I would find food, the spots I would swim to find oxygen. We'd wander along creeks and streams and gaze out over the water, peaceful and serene settings, and then would come my quiz: "Where do you see the fish, Cheryl?" Over time, I became a reader of water, and I would point to a spot. "There," I'd say, "they're right in there." In many ways, I believe I became more the fish than the fisherwoman. Gleaning insight into their habits, I joined them in their watery world.

I also learned to fish off a drift boat while the guide worked his ass off trying to help me cast well enough to catch a fish, untangled my lines, and pointed me to the best spots to cast. Often the guide would row the boat close enough to the spot where I might by some act of God hook a fish. Most of the time the guide was more concerned that I catch a fish than I was, as I continued my habit of happily gazing out over the river, deep in reverie. Through it all, John was calmly and deftly casting, catching, and releasing. We'd always pause to take a photo of his triumphs, and our photo albums include numerous shots of John proudly displaying his monumental fish. There are distinctly fewer shots featuring me doing the same.

In 1988, I stepped out of a plane and into Montana for the first time. Arriving from the congestion of urban Oakland, California, I felt my lungs expand in a clear air I was unused to breathing. Welcomed by the vast robin's-egg sky with its white mountains of clouds, I was carried into the wild blue yonder known as the Big Sky Country of Montana. Upon leaving the small Bozeman airport, I entered an open, spacious deliciousness that I had never known before in my life.

Several days later, John and I floated the Yellowstone River with a guide named Bill Flick, a slightly crusty older guy in a worn red plaid shirt and dusty brown waders who'd clearly seen a lot of action in his time. I was decked out in my overalls, waders, and the requisite fishing hat. I wore a dazzling and fashionable white baseball cap atop my long, dark curls—yet another faux pas, as I learned that the brightness of the cap was likely to catch the reflection of the sunlight and spook the fish. (Apparently, fish were far more sensitive and aware than I had previously given them credit for.) I was freezing cold, because you always have to set out at the crack of dawn, when the fish are hungry and the rest of the world hasn't arrived at the river yet.

Bill was the son of a man named Art Flick, best known for his book *Streamside Guide* (published in 1947) and for being a master flytier. Bill had published his own book in 1972, a volume titled *Master Fly-Tying Guide*. When John had told me about Bill and that we'd be fishing with him, he'd seemed as thrilled as he ever let himself be about anything. "Great!" I'd said, secretly hoping I wouldn't have to undertake the task of unpeeling my waders to pee in the scratchy bushes as we drifted down the Yellowstone River.

We were in the lush Paradise Valley, the Yellowstone cutting and winding between the rocky, darkly foreboding

Absaroka and Gallatin mountain ranges, as the sun began its ascent. It was October, so the grasses were still golden from the summer's heat and not yet killed off by the cover of the winter snows to come. Warmed by the heat, I finally thawed enough to stand in the front of the boat (the beginner's place) and begin trying my hand at fishing this notorious river. A man of few words, Bill did occasionally come out of his silence to correct my fishing techniques by telling me how to hold the rod, strip the line, and watch the bobber. "Set the hook, Cheryl, set the hook!" he would comment sternly as I jerked my line out of the water and back over my head. Bill's guidance of me probably required him to speak more than he was used to, and clearly more than he particularly enjoyed.

"Don't let your thumb flop like that," he said.

"Okay," I said, and my thumb promptly flopped again.

"No," Bill said, "like this," and then he demonstrated the correct way to hold my thumb against my rod.

"Oh, I see," I replied, and immediately repeated my bad casting habits again.

Meanwhile, John was rapidly pulling up a stunning variety of trout. By then, I was thinking more about the large glass of chardonnay I planned to have back at the dude ranch than these damn fish. But on we continued.

Finally, Bill lost his patience: "Cheryl, if you do that one more time, I'm going to cut off your thumb!"

Yikes!

At the end of a long day on the river, you always take a picture with your guide. In the photo from the Yellowstone River in 1988, you see me and Bill Flick grinning at the camera as if we're the best of fishing buddies—or maybe his wide grin is an indication of how happy and relieved he is just to get me out of his boat! It's important to note that I still have both thumbs in the shot.

John and I spent a good amount of time on the Sacramento River in California with a guide named Phil White, a round-faced, boyish, young father of two whose talkative nature and gift of storytelling made for good laughs. Phil let us know that "everything will be fine and we'll all get along on this boat as long as we agree not to talk politics." In the fly-fishing world, this usually meant that we were in the company of a staunch conservative who had taken one look at me and correctly assumed my liberal tendencies. *Okay, no problem*, I thought to myself.

During the time we spent with Phil, we went through two presidents, George W. and Obama, without incident. John, Phil, and I spent some great time together on what the fishermen call "the Lower Sac," not only fishing but also enjoying the Corn Nuts Phil always carried onboard.

"Phil will keep you entertained for sure," his online profile reads, and I can attest to the truth of this advertisement.

I've never had a guide row a boat harder than Phil did as he maneuvered up and down the river, putting me as close as possible to chunky steelhead. "You're really workin' off those Corn Nuts, man," I'd joke.

Between his dauntless rowing stints, Phil spent time doing what he called "knitting," which meant untangling the many and significant messes I made of my line throughout our float. He was the guide who actually helped me catch a number of fish, instructing me in the art of casting by demonstrating how to cast as if I had tiny *T. rex* arms, the purpose of which was to counteract my usually loose and ineffectual movements. He demonstrated the technique that first day by pulling his arms in close to his body, making little flaps out of his hands, and screeching, "EEEeeeee Errrrerrrr EEEeee!"

After watching him, I stood strong and ferocious in my beginner's spot at the front of the boat, imitating his moves and the sounds. "EEEeee, EEEeeee!" I shouted over the river.

In a rare moment of triumph, I caught more fish than John that day. I would utilize this technique for years to come.

Some of the most beautiful times I have had on a river were with Wayne Eng, who is known as a teaching fly-fishing guide. John and I spent time with Wayne in the Dunsmuir area of California, this time on the section of the Sacramento River known as the Upper Sac. My Zen master of fly-fishing, this gentle man with a long, dark ponytail, beautiful smile, and kind eyes beneath his floppy hat, gave me far beyond the experience of learning to fish. Wayne once told me, "*I believe my job is to help people catch fish by design, not by accident." He called this approach "streamsmithing."* To me, it meant properly reading the water and understanding where the fish might be, then crafting a presentation that would induce them to take the fly. Wayne would stand next to me in the stream and calmly talk me through every movement, our conversations philosophical and intimate. We'd stand together and look up at majestic Mount Shasta in a kind of reverent silence, and I would glimpse the simplicity of being with the natural world. Here, I could leave behind the complexity of my life and, like John, feel whole.

But after a while, even Wayne would remind me that we were here to fish and not just to blend into the natural world. We had a purpose.

He once took John and me to a little trout pond on private land because he so desperately wanted me to catch a fish and he knew that might just be the place. As usual, Wayne and I were just getting set up when John caught a gargantuan trout on his first cast. *Oh well*, I thought, *here we go again*. But moments later, I landed a fish!

By this fishing trip, I had enough experience to be left to my own devices, and Wayne, always the wise guide, mostly left me alone. I remember looking across the pond—the mountains looming around us, the green of the grasses surrounding us—and seeing Wayne and John talking. Their smiles, the way they seemed to share an intimacy rare for most men, would remain a memorable photograph in my mind.

John had scheduled our next guided trip with Wayne for June of 2016, but he died a month before the trip. I sent a message to Wayne, canceling the trip, and he responded with shock and sorrow.

Wayne is the only guide I can imagine ever going fishing with again. It's hard to fathom whether I'll be ready, but something within me is pulled to go to the place that was so very special to me and John and for one last time cast my line into the crystal, pure water of the Upper Sac with Wayne Eng by my side.

CHAPTER 9

*For thousands of years, father and son have stretched
wistful hands across the canyon of time . . .*
—ALAN VALENTINE

B en never took to fishing. As a small boy, he would
collect rocks by the side of the river and build tiny,
imaginary villages, absorbed in a fantasy world far away
from an impatient father whose desire for his son to love
fly-fishing was too demanding to allow his son the space
to choose to join him. John placed a beginner's rod in
small hands when Ben was too young to be able to handle
it, let alone work with some of the complexities of fishing.
Watching John try to make him sit still was excruciating,
and John's insistence that I stay out of their experience
only created more tension as our family struggled with
outings that were sometimes steeped not with fun but
with frustration.

I spent years caught between two males—my husband
and my son. Struggling with the impossible task of being in
the middle, and the inevitable betrayal experienced by both

of them, I became a stealthy mediator in the relationship of the two human beings I was most connected with and loved more than anything or anyone in the entire world. I don't believe that either one of them had any idea that this was a painful dilemma I felt trapped in. Certainly, Ben, as a child, was not responsible for understanding my feelings. But I wonder if, over the years, he harbored some resentment—not of his father but of me, for not always siding with him in jagged moments of disagreement and strife. I don't believe that John ever really grasped my plight or my sorrow, or the fact that I worked hard to negotiate this space in his relationship with his son. If he saw my pain, he never acknowledged what it meant for me to stagger back and forth between them, always conscious of not lingering too long on one side or the other. So dogged in his stubborn and wounded need for recognition and for an end to the loneliness he himself had endured as a child, he was too close to the fire to feel the heat of the hurt. John used to say to Ben, "When you're gone and on your own, I'll still be here with your mother." What an ironic and cruel lie that proved to be.

When Ben was around eight years old, we made a trip to the California Delta to picnic and fish for catfish. This wasn't fly-fishing but bait fishing, with a spinner. It was hot and uncomfortable; rickety picnic tables with splinters dotted a mottled brown grassy space with very little shade. My skin, slathered in sunscreen, felt sticky.

Ben did land a catfish on this trip. The deal was always that if you caught something, you needed to kill it yourself, and then you had to eat the fish you sacrificed for your own need. Not on any endangered species list, catfish, a primitive creature reminiscent of cockroaches, will likely continue to exist forever, regardless of earth's demise. John had brought a hammer and a small nail; we used those to puncture the prehistoric catfish through its meaty head, and John sat by Ben as he bravely smacked the fish. I looked on and then, because I had also hauled up one of these bizarre creatures, had to punch my catch through the head too.

As much as Ben and I struggled with this, I appreciated the lesson behind the murderous action that John was teaching his son. We weren't buying fish in plastic wrap, all nicely cleaned up and ready to eat. In the native tradition, we were honoring the sacrifice the fish had made for our benefit. In the fly-fishing world, "You kill it, you eat it." In today's technological world, we've become so mesmerized by virtual reality that these rites of passage for boys learning to be men have largely disappeared into the computerized graphics of fantasy environments.

We also traveled to Lake Tahoe each year and fished in secluded spots John had scouted out that would accommodate a child. We'd hike dusty and sweet-smelling trails to small, sparkling streams shaded by the fragrant branches of giant pines and serenaded by the whisper of the shivering leaves of aspens. John would carefully put together our fishing gear and pack us lunches to enjoy as we sat on rocks and logs far away from video games and the intrusion of television. The pressure to learn to fish seemed to matter less in these sanctuaries as the natural world enveloped us like a deep breath. One such outing included a small chipmunk we named Chip in a flare of originality. Chip benefited from our lunch and greatly enjoyed the grapes he allowed us to give him. Nature, in its wisdom, provided peace and spaciousness and gave us respite from our human foibles.

In 2012, a decade after these early attempts to entice Ben into a love of fishing, John and I traveled to Lees Ferry at the mouth of the Colorado River with a guide named Terry Gunn and set out on a boat for a cruise through Marble Canyon. By now, Ben was in college and John had given up inviting him along on fishing expeditions; the hope of a father-son alliance around fly-fishing had waned long ago. Gazing up at the eroded, millions-of-years-old Vermilion Cliffs rising three thousand feet from the base of the river, I admired how the light of the Southwest sun on these magnificent, steep cliffs glowed red-orange in the early-morning light beneath an iris blue, cloudless sky. Terry told us about his own son and their shared love of fishing. He never placed a rod in his son's hands, only brought him along when he went fishing and brought spare rods along, leaving them around on the ground or against a tree. He waited for his son to pick up the rod himself— which, eventually, his boy did, making the choice of learning to fish about his own curiosity and not his father's dream. In this moment, John acknowledged the mistakes he had made with his own son, and disappointment started to make its way through regret to acceptance. "I pushed too hard, too early," he said in a quiet voice, and then he grew silent. Nothing more was said, and on we went, down the river . . . floating into one of the best days of fishing we ever had.

Three years after the Lees Ferry trip and a decade after the end of these infamous family fishing expeditions, Ben moved into his first apartment. It was 2015, the beginning of his senior year at UCLA. In a great stroke of chaotic fortune, a stupid and unnecessary argument at a restaurant blew open the years of conflict between John and Ben. John lost his temper and stormed out ahead of Ben and me. Once again, my heart threw itself against my chest, and my stomach clenched with a sick anxiety and my own anger. I took the steady role but this time stayed with Ben. The fight had begun with some innocuous remark from Ben that had triggered John's frustration, which escalated into a full-blown, uncontrolled tirade. Like most arguments, these incidents rarely made any sense and most always served to rip open a torrent of confusing thoughts and emotions wrapped in hurtful words.

After John's furious departure, I paid the bill while the grizzled old Italian waiter pretended not to have noticed the disruption at his table. Ben and I left on our own, and I silently wondered if we should go to the car, walk, or call a cab to pick us up. When we reached the car, John was waiting and had somewhat cooled off. But in seconds, they both burst into flames again, and after a hellish several minutes, I took the risk of asking if I might say what I saw, what I felt was happening. For the first time, John's strangled reply was, "Please." I was finally allowed to speak openly about what I saw, what I knew, and after I was finished, the two of them had the conversation that had been waiting to happen for years. Agonizing and heartbreaking words were spoken by both of them. Emotions that had been buried barely beneath their surfaces poured out into the hot Los Angeles night, carried along by tears and fury. The relationship broke open in a torrent of love that had lived for too long in an agony of miscommunication and misunderstanding. As they both caught fire, I witnessed a new beginning.

Less than a year later, on the night before John died, Ben and John had their final conversation. Ben's honor's thesis in history had been chosen for an award, and he had presented his poster earlier that day. He was excitedly calling to tell us about his experience. By this point in time, John had taken interest in some of the things that most mattered to Ben as a way to connect with the son he loved so deeply. Their relationship, while still prone to storms, was evolving. Their last moments were filled with laughter, love, and, perhaps most importantly, respect, and I am profoundly grateful for my son that this was the case, as less than twelve hours later, his father was dead.

CHAPTER 10

*Angling expertise is a highly coordinated
synthesis of skillful casting, imaginative
stalking, keen vision, quick reflexes, plenty of
savvy and lots of experience.*
—SHERIDAN ANDERSON

fly-fishing
noun: the sport (art) of fishing using a rod and an artificial fly as bait

Basic Fly-Fishing Equipment
- a fly rod
- a fly reel
- fly-fishing line, which consists of: backing, fly line, a leader, and a tippet
- a few flies, of course; hard to fly-fish without flies!

*The best thing about fishing is that it
takes place entirely in the present tense . . .*
—JOHN GIERACH

What could be so hard about this?
—CHERYL KRAUTER

As the years went by, I became less of an observer and more of a participant in the fly-fishing world. I would be lying if I said that I ever became a seasoned veteran among those who live and breathe for those moments on the stream—yet lying is an enormous part of the fishing culture. The lying, bragging, and competitive spirit reaches great heights in particular during the debriefs that happen at the end of a day fishing on the river. There's a saying that goes, "It's amazing how big the fish got by the time you get back to the car." By the time you get back to your cabin, the fish has become Moby Dick.

John and I were fishing in a favorite hole on the Truckee River in Northern California when another fisherman passed us walking on the cliff above the river. It is stream etiquette to ask, "How's the fishing?" John asked the requisite question, and the guy immediately told us he was having one of his best days ever and stretched his arms straight out from his body to indicate that he had basically caught a fish the size of a shark.

"Great!" we said, congratulating him on his success.

That gesture became a favorite between us from that day on whenever either of us caught a fish. Based on years of observation, my humble opinion is that one of the most essential skills in fly-fishing is to perfect the "Big Lie," thereby earning respect and admiration from your fellow fly-fishers.

Orvis, a family-owned business founded in 1856 to sell fishing tackle, updated in modern times with a website that also provides fly-fishing tips, writes, "Casting is one of the great aspects of fly fishing. Many find the rhythmic motion is relaxing and even therapeutic. Like other activities, such as golf or tennis, you need to learn the essentials and practice in order to achieve success. But the key is that it's easy to learn." The part that's true about this statement is that casting a fly rod is indeed like swinging a tennis racket. When you watch the pros do it, it looks smooth and easy—but for the rest of us, there's so much that can go wrong.

Casting well enough to hook a fish depends on accuracy and a certain unforced gracefulness, plus a lot of power. Frankly, it's a lot to put together while you're struggling to keep your balance in a stream or on a boat while simultaneously being told to "let your rod do the work" and create a dynamic casting arc. Casting arcs are the arc the rod makes in the air during the cast, and the arc of a strong cast is the path that the fly rod follows during a complete (meaning successful) cast. In fly-fishing, being able to create this arc with your cast means you've placed your fly exactly where you wanted it to go and into the mouth of an awaiting trout. I have witnessed perfect, ascendant moments of arc when John would cast his line alongside me, often after I had been fishing a spot for a good amount of time, and in one movement, find a fish. I'd like to say that I felt congratulatory when that happened, but that would just be another example of lying while fishing.

None of the fish we caught while fly-fishing ever saw the inside of a frying pan or landed on a grill. Like most avid and committed fly-fishers, we practiced catch-and-release fishing. Catch-and-release is a custom within recreational fishing intended as a technique of conservation. Many of today's rivers only allow catch-and-release fishing to preserve these remarkable, beautiful creatures. The hooks are barbless, and, after capture, the fish are held in the water (sometimes in a net equipped with a measure to ensure at least some sense of accuracy for the bragging and lying that will later take place), sized up, and then released. As John used to say, "You don't eat the baseball."

Catch-and-release reminds me of how we attach to one another and the inevitable ways in which we must then let go of those we have brought closer than we ever believed possible. As babies, it's essential that we attach to a loving figure and that the same loving figure attaches to us. We form a strong bond, and then, eventually, if all goes well, we let go. Children grow up.

Intimate relationships, without this bond, will break apart. But in the end, we all leave or are left. The sparkling golden hues of a large trout surges upstream away from us and is gone. The ones we love are here, and then they're not.

Stalking is, literally, sneaking up on the fish. Stooping, crawling, hiding behind rocks and bushes, the stealthy fly fisherman becomes the cunning and clever hunter of his quarry. The art of stalking is to stay low and to be as quiet as possible while crawling on your knees to avoid spooking the fish you are seeking. This is not something you see on the cover of fly-fishing magazines or books, and I do not recall watching the dashing stars of fly-fishing movies clamber around on their knees.

Stalking is supposed to help you be where the fish are without them taking notice of you. I have dragged myself along the ground on my hands and knees and hidden behind the aforementioned rocks and bushes (this particular technique did not go very well for me, as I hooked more bushes than fish on that outing), but my most stellar stalking experience happened on the Truckee River.

On that day, after carefully stalking a likely spot, I quietly waded into the river. The brisk water was clear enough to see to the bottom—where, at one point, at least a dozen unconcerned fish swam all around me, seeming not to feel the least bit in danger of my presence.

Although I cast my line many times, in the end I did not hook any of them. These old, seasoned trout may have recognized a novice fly-fisher and chosen to stay close by rather than risk being hooked by my experienced husband, who was fishing only yards away. In fly-fishing lingo, the fish circling around your feet while you cast wildly about is called "the fish flipping you the fin."

Rivers know this: There is no hurry.
We shall get there someday.
—A. A. Milne

Reading water means being able to determine the most likely places you will find holding or cruising fish. Be a stealthy observer: as you stalk the water, stop well back from the edge, and stay still until you can be sure that you won't spook any fish before you get a chance to cast to them. As you scan the water before you, make your mind into that of a fish and look for the three things that fish crave: cover, food, and margins. *Cover* includes weed beds, fallen trees, overhanging vegetation, or rock, and offers shelter from both animal and human predators. *Food* can be in the form of schools of bait or insects on the water or along the banks. And fish like to hang in *margins*—the edges between deep water and shallow water, fast water and slow water, or cover and open water. Wherever there is current, in a river or the ocean, fish will seek places where they can hold still in slower water while allowing faster currents to deliver food to them. Like all living creatures, they seek shelter, rest, and security.

I found shelter, rest, and security with John. I enjoy fishing, but what I really enjoyed was being with John in his element, gazing over a river or stream in search of "fishy water," sharing a quiet moment side by side. I'd give anything to have more time with him, sitting on a log or looking down from a cliff at the water. I have come to understand that I, too, live in the margins now, roaming the edge between the deep and shallow water of my soul. I've become an underwater creature in the silent turbulence of my grief.

CHAPTER 11

You say you're going fishing all the time,
well I'm going fishing too.
You can bet your life your loving wife
is gonna catch as many fish as you.
Now you say you're always fishing when you stay out late,
well here's a little something that your wife's gonna state:
There's plenty fish will bite if you've got good bait,
so I'm going fishing too.
—CHRIS SMITH

On July 14, 2017, I step out of a plane and into Montana for the second time. Twenty-nine years have passed since John and I landed in this same airport, and much looks the same, but much has changed, too. In 1988, the plane doors opened to a metal stairway and there was nothing but Montana sky in the distance. In 2017, I stroll down a carpeted jetway and into the airport—where craft beers and upscale artwork are now sold—and have to take the escalator down to baggage claim before I get to glimpse the openness of Big Sky Country. The bronze fly fisherman, however, faithful dog forever by his side, is still in midcast, his line flowing above the grassy spot of land in front of Bozeman Yellowstone International Airport. The statue, frozen in time, shows very little signs of age, whereas I have been touched by the past decades—my once long, curly black hair now short and gray, a few more lines on my face. I have my Montana fishing license, but unlike in 1988, I carry no fishing rods. I arrive alone with John's ashes, bringing him to the place where he always wanted to return.

I've arrived in Montana to float in a small boat down the Madison River. I am in hiking boots, while John, a chalky mixture of ash and small bits of bone, is tucked in my carry-on. I pick up my car and drive off down a deserted and lonely road, traveling to where I will fish and then leave his ashes behind in a beautiful, sacred river full of trout, as I promised him I would.

I begin my drive with a surreal, sickened feeling in the pit of the stomach, following directions I've entered in my GPS and with no real idea of where I am heading in this remote southwest corner of Montana. I've always enjoyed traveling to places that are foreign to me, often with far less of a plan than I have today, but I'm older now than in my earlier solo-traveling days and no longer used to setting off on my own without a partner—without John. As I drive along the deserted highway I feel afraid and lonely realizing that I am in an unknown place where no one knows who I am or where I am. It's hard to tell whether my shortness of breath and constricted throat is related to anxiety or sorrow. I'm talking to myself out loud in the car, asking, "Why are you here, why are you doing this?"

I'm making my way to Rainbow Valley Lodge in Ennis, Montana, speeding down deserted roads with no designated speed limits across a hot, golden land whose feathery growth sways in a strong wind, burnt from the relentless sun. I am often the only car on the road. Herds of cows pay little attention as I wonder if I am going the right way, thinking to myself, *Where the hell am I?* I have to trust that the annoying voice coming from my phone will get me to this tiny town with a population so small that the percentage can't even be measured against the population of where I'm coming from.

After a while, water comes into view along the road, some small, meandering streams and some large, rushing rivers. Occasionally, I see a small boat floating along, fishermen casting their lines into the water. I notice other fishermen wading in the streams, others on the banks. A sign announcing that I am crossing the Madison River appears on the highway and—I take a deep breath—I know I'm on the right track. Highway 84 out of Norris, Montana (a stop consisting of a gas station, a furniture outlet, and a hot spring called the Water of the Gods), dead-ends, and I turn left onto US 287 South, bound for my destination in the searing, windy, dramatic country known as the Madison River Valley.

Welcome to Ennis, Montana—population 840 people, eleven million trout. Well, okay, even I should be able to land a few trout here! Prior to the arrival of Europeans, the Shoshone, Flathead, and Bannock tribes hunted the Madison Valley each spring, but as I drive down the main—and only—street in Ennis, there are no signs that the original people who lived here ever existed. The long-ago decimated American Indian culture of this Montana valley is invisible among the bars and fly-fishing shops and the whiskey distillery where tourists line up for a shot.

I stop to sit outside and have a beer in a local beer-and-burger joint, and as I sip I watch members of a familiar fishing culture all around me. Well-dressed white men in khaki fishing shirts and equipped with expensive gear whose brand names are well-known to me are sitting separately from the local guides, who wear jeans, T-shirts, the occasional cowboy shirt, and well-worn fishing hats. Clothes do not make the fisherman, and I have no doubt as to which members of this crowd are the real experts with a rod. The groups of well-clad men gather around cell phone photographs to compete over the "catch of the day," while the rugged guides who've steered and busted their asses helping them all day laugh over beers at tables nearby.

Beer finished, I head to Rainbow Valley Lodge, located just outside of town, where I meet the owner, Ed, a big, soft bear of a man who greets me with a wonderful kindness when I introduce myself. He and his wife, Jeanne, donated this trip and a two-night stay at their place to the Casting for Recovery raffle. They are familiar with the story of how I have come to be here this summer, a year after John's death. From this first moment, in his quiet and unobtrusive way, Ed begins looking after me. He will continue to do so during my entire stay at Rainbow Valley Lodge.

After I check into my room, I realize I need to ask Ed a question, so I head back toward the office. I find Ed sitting outside with a group of men, having an early-evening beer. I notice Ed turning to the small group of men as I come closer, and I realize he is telling them my story, because their eyes dart between me and Ed as they listen to him talk, and when they look up as I stop in front of them, their faces are painted with a mixture of discomfort and pain. They barely manage to mumble hello when Ed introduces me, and they make minimal eye contact before they look away. I imagine they are concerned that I may grow emotional before their very eyes, which is not a welcome sight at a fly-fishing lodge in Montana.

Another lively group of men lounges outside their rooms, laughing and drinking. They've brought an enormous barbecue with the Jack Daniel's logo on its side. I learn that one of them is, indeed, the owner of Jack Daniel's, and that this same group of guys makes an annual pilgrimage to Rainbow Valley Lodge. The Jack Daniel's group looks like a lot of fun, but every time I pass by them, the conversation and laughter immediately stops and they grow silent. I coulda really enjoyed a shot of Jack with them, but I'm beginning to understand that my presence is a bit frightening to these guys who've traveled a long way to let go of whatever troubles exist in their world.

That night, before the fishing trip I'm here to take, I dream that I am with my good friend Sandra. We are going someplace, and I am at her house. She has a window ledge where she's placed golden rocks and crystals of different shapes and sizes, very beautiful and arranged in a perfectly stunning design. We're about to go, and I say to her, "What about John? Aren't we going to have John come with us?" I'm upset that we're not waiting for him, but she turns away without a word.

When I wake up, I realize that John is not here, he's not in Montana—in fact, he's not anywhere. I'm here alone.

The morning of the trip, I put my fishing clothes on. It's hot and we'll be in a boat so, thank God, I didn't have to bring the waders. I'm wearing my old fishin' jeans and a fishing shirt John bought me just before a trip we planned together that did not happen. I've proudly donned my Casting for Recovery cap, which is adorned with my cancer survivor buttons.

At seven in the morning, the heat is already scathing and there's a bit too much wind. Heavy clouds start to gather, threatening thunderstorms. Guides are arriving, boats in tow, trucks parked in the gravel lot, and there's much banter between them as they size up their clients. The ever-thoughtful Ed is waiting in the lobby so he can introduce me to the guide who will take me out.

Mike "Dirty Mike" Elliot, my guide on the Madison River, is a young mountain man who's been assigned to take me on this half-day float trip. He pulls up with a battered boat and a truck that looks like it's seen some rough miles. I overhear some of the other guides joking about the cows he's run into, or that have run into him, as they look at the dents in his truck.

Mike emerges in a well-worn, probably favorite, red plaid shirt. His fishing hat looks like something has chewed on the edges of it, and there are bits of feathers, or straw, on the band. He doesn't look all the way to sullen but is pretty close—although he's hard to read with those dark glasses covering his eyes.

I'm in the breakfast room, chewing on some oatmeal made from a packet that I have overmicrowaved and sipping on some juice, avoiding the sweet rolls that are the usual fare of the motel continental breakfast. I have John's ashes in my small pack, and I'm wondering if my guide will be amenable to me spreading them along the river as we fish.

Ed introduces us. Mike takes one look at me, barely says hello, and heads back to his boat.

Uh-oh, I think, *this may be a long damn day*. His attitude has suggested that, after one glance, he's decided he doesn't want to deal with some old lady who probably doesn't know the first thing about fly-fishing. This assumption is annoying, because it's taken years of practice and lessons from other guides to get to where I am today in fly-fishing. I'm put off by his attitude and begin to wonder what the hell kind of experience this is going to be, sitting alone in a boat with a guide who looks like he'd rather be just about anywhere else than with me on a river for hours. This actually may be the one thing that connects us in these first few moments of our time together.

We head off in Mike's truck. I wonder if I'll need to sit by the boat while he moves the car to the spot where we'll put in after our float. But he has another person who will take care of bringing the truck to where we will end up much later today. It's hot, and apparently the fish haven't been too active during the past few days. Mike is watching the wind and the weather; there's no shelter along the river, and that makes for some understandable concern about lightning striking, especially since we sit in a metal boat.

Mike doesn't like crowds and tells me that we'll head off to a less popular section of the Madison River so as to avoid other fishermen. I notice that he's only brought along one rod, which is unusual; in my experience the guide usually carries a couple of rods so that we can adjust to the fishing as we go. Also, he has no idea of my experience level, which means he selected a single rod based solely on what assumptions he's made about me, knowing nothing about me or my skill set. I'm used to being contacted by the guide prior to a fishing trip so that he can assess what I know and what I can do. This short check-in might have introduced me as someone who, while not an expert, knew what she was doing. *Oh well*, I think, *here we go.*

As we meander along on our float, we talk about how I happen to be here, and I tell him that I've fished over the years with my husband, who was a master fly fisherman. Mike brightens at this news, skipping quickly over the past tense: *was* a master fly fisherman. Figuring that he hasn't heard that my husband is dead, I tell him, "My husband died. It was his raffle ticket that won this trip, but he died before it was drawn."

Dirty Mike doesn't know what to do with this information, so he says nothing and we float silently down the Madison River on our way to the fishing spots he has scouted. At this point, I realize that I will be wandering away from the boat at some point during the day for a private ritual of scattering the ashes. Ole Dirty Mike is not going to be the boatman from the River Styx, and I don't need his blessing to scatter John's ashes.

We arrive at our first spot, and Mike sets me up with his battered rod and puts me at the front of the boat. I begin casting . . . and soon, I begin catching. Mike perks up and I can almost see the wheels in his brain starting to turn in a different direction. He must be wondering if the day will not be quite as long and tedious as he first believed it might be. Perhaps he's thinking, *Maybe this old lady knows a bit about what she's doing.* On occasion, he congratulates me on a good cast. He also begins to teach me the ways of fly-fishing the Madison.

Whenever other boats and guides make their way down the river past us, Mike stops the boat and heads to the bank to wait for them to pass, making sure we are always alone on our own little stretch of the river. He doesn't seem the social type, but I'm beginning to sense that he's also committed to bringing me to the most isolated, least fished sections of the river—to giving me the best experience possible. I watch the other fishermen in their boats, some of them laughing and telling stories. On the other boats there is a mood of hilarity, but this is not the case with Dirty Mike. We remain quiet, yet the silence isn't uncomfortable or forced. I'm still thinking about how to leave the ashes along the route when he comes back from a bathroom break and tells me that it isn't such a good idea for me to get out in the grasses, as he has seen some pretty big rattlesnakes recently. *Well, that settles that,* I think. Luckily, for the moment, I don't have to go.

In one of our shared silent reveries, I spot familiar-looking birds flying about us.

"Are those seagulls?" I ask Mike, astonished at keeping company with a flock of California seagulls on the Madison River, far from their Pacific Ocean habitat.

"Yes," he tells me, letting me know that the seagull is, indeed, quite a common bird in this territory.

As I watch them soar and listen to their squawks, I marvel at the surprising connectedness of nature, one that places gulls on the sand of the California beaches I know so well and then sends them soaring over the rivers of Montana, where I now sit in a small boat, far from all that is known to me.

While Mike is a man of few words, as we continue on our little journey, we begin to talk more. What happens is familiar. I become the listener; he tells his story, and I ask questions that open up a conversation. His is an interesting story, one that is a far cry from my own. It reminds me of my childhood fascination with the Little House on the Prairie books. As a child in the Pacific Northwest, I would pretend to be Laura, who lived on the prairie—and now I am with someone who really *is* from the prairie.

He grew up here in Montana. He hunts, fishes, and works on a ranch during the brutal winters in this remote valley. He hunts elk and other game that he dresses, butchers, and preserves himself. When people come for dinner, they are excited to eat what he has hunted and prepared but he, in truth, longs for a pork chop bought at the only market in the area.

Slowly, I learn about Mike, his girlfriend. She is the editor of the local paper, and he is clearly so enamored of her that in an instant he endears himself to me. She spent many childhood summers in Montana, and after schooling in the East, she came west to work for the small newspaper in the valley. His pride in her is very touching, indeed, and reminds me of how John always expressed his pride in me.

Mike tells me about an upcoming wedding they're going to in the Hamptons. He is, quite naturally, nervous, as he doesn't know what to expect.

"I'm used to wearing jeans and my cowboy hat to parties and events," he tells me.

Uh-oh, I think, looking at that raggedy hat with its different flies and even a stalk of what appears to be wheat stuck in the hatband. During our float, he picks up a feather and tucks it into the band alongside the wheat.

"You know," I say, "it's possible to rent a suit or tuxedo for the wedding. And you might want to consider leaving your hat behind."

After five hours on the Madison River, we finish a successful day of fishing. I've caught the most and the biggest fish
I've ever caught in my life. These big babies stayed behind
in the river, carefully released back into their watery territory—still free. Mike hauls the boat out of the river and
hooks it back up to that well-used truck, and we head back
to Rainbow Valley Lodge. On our way, he takes me by his
house to show me where he lives, and we talk about what
the winter will be like in Montana when the fishing season
ends. He'll hunt, tie some flies for the next season. I think
to myself, *While you're snowed in and waiting out the winter,
I'll be in California waiting and hoping for rain, working with
cancer patients, writing books.*

We are two people from worlds that do not touch each
other. There is no possibility that we would ever be friends or
even casual acquaintances, or that our paths will ever cross
again. Our lives are lived in completely different places, and
its likely for the best that our politics and belief systems
were left quiet as we sat together and floated today. But for
this half-day on a majestic river, we have been companions.

While I'd like to believe that we both left some mark
on each other, I have no doubt that Mike will quickly forget
me. I, on the other hand, will always remember him as the
young man I spent a day with on the Madison River in
Montana who in my memory will never grow old.

In the end, Mike and I were perfect companions on
our journey today. We gave each other the gift of silence—
allowed each other a chance for reflection. I don't know
what he felt or thought along the way, but the quiet gave

me the space to think of John and take in the scene before me, almost as if he were along on the trip he won. My inner dialogue became a conversation with him, describing the world I was floating through and proudly showing him the fish I caught.

Somewhere along one of the bends of that ancient river, I realized that today's trip was not the time or place to scatter John's ashes. It is not an act to perform quickly or carelessly, and I need to be alone when I do it—just me and John in our final moment together.

Later that day at the farm-to-table dinner at Rainbow Valley Lodge, I sit next to a lovely man who tells me that he and five other men meet here every year to fish together. They are professional, accomplished men who come from different places across America.

"What are you doing here?" he asks me.

"I came to fish," I say. "I spent today on the river."

"Oh, that was you on the river today!" he exclaims.

"Yes, with a guide," I reply.

He goes on to tell me how they saw me today and all noticed that I could actually fish.

"Your casting is quite good," he tells me. "We were all watching you."

"Thanks," I say, honored by the compliment.

"You know," he tells me, "all of these guys' wives are at home while they've gone fishing. They don't know what to do with a woman who can fly-fish."

Feeling like he might be receptive to my story, I tell him about what brought me here. I get teary, and in response he also tears up and reaches for my hand. We have a little moment, it's lovely, and then it passes. He turns to his friends and I turn back to my dessert.

❧

After dinner, when I return to my room, once again passing the Jack Daniel's cohort who, once again, goes silent, I understand why they avert their eyes. I am a woman who can fish, a grieving widow, a reminder of all they have come here to forget. Back in the solitariness of my room, I weep alone.

If all goes well over the next year, the Jack Daniel's gang and my kind dinner companion and his friends will gather again to enjoy friendship far away from their wives and daily lives. They will join with one another in the joy of being on one of the great fly-fishing rivers in the world. They will laugh with one another and lie about the fish that they have caught. And then time will pass, as it does, and there will be other fishermen who will take their places in this annual ritual—fishermen bonding with one another and connecting with the natural world and the genetics of the hunter woven into their DNA.

I, in contrast—the woman, the gatherer of stories—know that this pilgrimage will be my last. I will not come this way again.

CHAPTER 12

The wind shows us how close to the edge we are.
—JOAN DIDION

The day after my fishing expedition, I go off in search for a place to scatter John's ashes. I've got a whole day, so I decide to drive up to Yellowstone Park to visit and, perhaps, find a spot to have this one-guest funeral.

The road to Yellowstone winds along stretches where the river is wide, the current strong, and the way down steep and inaccessible. Fishermen out in boats, or by the side of the river, make these places too exposed, too public. The heat makes shimmering patterns on the road, and there's heaviness in the air that signals a summer storm on its way. At each turn, each bend, my eyes explore the terrain, looking for the place to fulfill my promise.

As I drive on, I figure I might as well do the tourist thing, seeing as I am heading for one of the most beautiful national parks in the country. Yellowstone National Park, established in 1872, was America's first national park, and to this day it remains one of our most popular, with millions of annual visitors. Immortalized in photographs and films, and represented by the iconic Yogi Bear, who made his home in "Jellystone Park," Yellowstone spans almost thirty-five hundred miles. While mostly in Wyoming, it extends into parts of Montana and Idaho as well, making it the eighth-largest national park in the US.

As I make my way to one of the world's most popular vacation and recreation locales, I am struck by the oddness of this journey, a moment in time that weaves together a guided fly-fishing half-day float trip down a mighty river, being with thousands of tourists at Yellowstone Park, and searching for a place to scatter my dead husband's ashes. Not your typical day.

Some days are more like entire eras. Linear time ceases, and emotions, along with the scenery, blend into a surreal, circular inner feeling that's both soothing and bizarre. Soon, I find myself walking through multicolored psychedelic geyser fields with hordes of people, all of them oohing and aahing and taking pictures. The heat is scorching, but, undaunted, I plow along with the crowds from one awesome sight to another.

I'm alone among the families and the couples. For a moment, I marvel at the enormous group of Japanese tourists pouring out of sleek, air-conditioned buses. They're like a stream of liquid silk spilling onto the dusty, gritty, steaming path that takes us all through the geyser field. Suddenly I feel lost, as though I am the only solo explorer in this hot and crowded conglomeration of humanity. I am starkly reminded of my aloneness in the midst of various groups joined together, laughing and talking with one another.

Having come this far, I decide to go all the way to the big daddy of geysers, Old Faithful. Apparently, Old

Faithful, true to its name, spews predictably enough that there are scheduled times to observe it blow. Equally predictable are the crowds that begin to gather for this event, making the restaurants and cafés nearly as inaccessible as the fishing spots I saw on the Madison River. Hunger wins out, however, and I enter the café that serves bison burgers—because, after all, what else would I eat in Montana? But the line is too long and I will miss Old Faithful if I wait, so I grab an expensive, premade, soggy-looking salad in one of the many gift shops and head outside again.

I perch on a butt-poking log next to a woman from Ohio who comes every year with her husband to the same spot. She chatters on about their motor home and the grandkids while I debate whether or not to tell her that I've brought my husband and he's sitting in the passenger seat of my rental car in a plastic bag. All things considered, I think better of sharing.

Rather anticlimactically, Old Faithful goes off at the appointed time, and almost automatically all of us spectators wander off to the next attraction.

I remember that when John and I came here in 1988, we went to an outlook over a deep gorge where a spectacular waterfall raged down steep cliffs into the river. I recall the roaring reverberation of the massive flow of water cascading into the pools below, drowning out people's conversations despite the distance between the falls and the outlook. There's a picture of me from that trip leaning against the fence post, my back to the waterfall, dark, curly hair past my shoulders, no eyeglasses, in a long, blue-striped shirt. My smile as I look at John is playfully seductive.

I decide I need to go back there, which means I have to find an information center, because I don't know where it is. An older woman, about my age, kindly pulls out a map when I tell her my story. She takes her time and, with enough description from me, outlines the spot on the map.

Pushing and dodging my way through literally thousands of people, I find my car—parked in a blessed shady spot—say hi to John's ashes on the passenger seat, noting that even in this cooler spot they are decidedly toastier than a few hours ago, and start the engine.

I get turned around multiple times as I attempt my exit from the seemingly endless maze of Yellowstone parking lots, which are now packed with cars, motorcycles, campers of all sizes, and, of course, the ubiquitous tour buses. I finally manage to stop going around in frustrating circles, find a way out of the maze, and start up the road toward Upper Falls.

The vast expanses of this place could swallow me whole; I drive past stunning vistas of rugged beauty with one eye on the road, the other continually looking for the signs leading to the falls. After several miles, I pull over, park, and head toward a wooden deck aged by decades of storms and snows that serves as an outlook.

Although the trip to the falls has taken less than thirty minutes, I experience another timeless moment as I walk to end of the spot overlooking the falls. I stand, silent and alone, allowing the sound of the roaring water to penetrate my body and soul.

There's an eternal sense of the power of the river as it surges over precipitous edges of the falls and crashes back into itself below. Somehow, it seems no different than it was twenty-nine years ago. Nothing has been brought in to change the landscape here. No fast-food restaurants or places to buy fancy coffees, no gift stores filled with expensive trinkets that will end up lost or forgotten. Still, it is not the same waterfall as it was even yesterday, let alone nearly thirty years ago. Nature is not static; the ecosystem shifts daily and, over hundreds and thousands of years, transforms all it touches. In the decades since my first visit, I, too, have been changed, not only by forces of nature but also by life circumstances—some chosen, others thrust upon me without regard for my plans.

I begin looking about for someone I might ask to take a photo of me. Feeling shy, I choose a woman standing nearby who looks about my age if she would mind taking my picture in the same spot where I stood twenty-nine years ago. The shot in 2017 shows a woman with short, spiky gray hair, glasses, and a silk shirt decorated with koi. You can recognize the shadow of the young woman reflected in the smile of the older woman—perhaps a bit more wistful, but still with a touch of sass.

The clouds begin to move faster as the wind picks up. The air swirls with heat that grows cooler as the volatile sky begins to darken. I've stalled long enough; it's time to find a burial site for John's ashes. Reluctantly, I leave and start my journey from Upper Falls in search of the place where I will scatter them.

As I drive back through the vast parkland of Yellowstone, I spot several small streams, the kind of water John loved to fish. At each stream, when a space to pull over appears, I do so, and then I get out to scout the location.

I get out of my car several times and stroll over to the edge of a few rivers and small streams, but none of them seems right—too many people around, the entry to the river too steep—and then it dawns on me that I am in Wyoming and that I must return to the part of the Madison River that flows through Montana, because that's what John would have wanted.

Continuing on, I see roiling black clouds up ahead on the road. An ominous darkness seems to follow me in every direction, and I suddenly feel as if I am in a race against a tempest that is waiting to engulf me as I speed down the nearly deserted road, wanting to make it back to Montana before being swept away in the deluge.

I'm driving through a valley surrounded by mountains. Shadows form on the sides of their peaks. They're frighteningly beautiful, and foreboding.

The rain starts slowly, but in what seems like minutes, it becomes torrential. I increase the speed of the wipers and try to breathe steadily as an edge of panic begins to take hold of me. My rental car is not the requisite large truck driven by those who live here, and I grip the wheel, at times struggling with steering, as the squall pounds on the roof and windows, threatening to derail my mission.

When the full force of the storm hits, I feel like my car is being propelled down the country road by the strong gusts of the winds that are chasing me and trying to overtake my expedition. Obsessive images of tornado chasers swirl around in my brain as the force of the storm follows me and I try to drive ahead of it. I am driving through a gale of rain, windshield wipers on full blast. Visibility becomes so clouded that at times I cannot see more than a few feet ahead of the car. Insanely, I drive over the speed limit, anticipating that I may actually start to fly.

As swiftly and severely as it began, the rain abruptly stops. Once I pass into Montana, I begin searching for places by the Madison River. I feel desperate, chaotic; a different, deeper aloneness clutches at my chest as my heartbeat flips around. I keep obsessively pulling off the highway to more secluded places, and then I become frightened of what might lurk in the dense brush and the abandoned ground by the river. I feel no sense of personal safety in the wildness of the storm, the countryside of Montana, combating the fierceness of my own volatile emotions. I don't want to be here. I want no part of my grief, my loss, the exhaustion of holding my life together through it all.

Please, please, make this all some nightmare that will end with John waking me and saying, "It's okay, you're dreaming."

I keep pulling off onto small dirt roads, following the river, but nothing seems right. The torrential rains and blustery winds have now given way to the heat of a scorching sun. Moment to moment, the changing weather seems to parallel my emotions as I scour the land for a place to scatter John's ashes.

Then a voice comes to me, saying, "I will guide you. I will tell you where you need to go."

Where is this coming from? Some place of knowledge within me? Is it John talking me through this, pointing out the way? Have I totally lost whatever shred of sanity I possessed before embarking on this odyssey?

At first, I ignore the voice and continue my relentless search—stopping the car, starting it again, stopping, starting, going nowhere. But the more insistently I disregard the voice, the louder it becomes. "I told you, I will tell you where to turn, where you will find the spot!" it shouts. Then, finally, annoyed and frustrated, it says, "This is how it always is, you never listen to me."

This phrase, delivered in this tone of voice, is unmistakably John's.

Some believe our loved ones watch over us, that they do not really leave us when they die but remain in contact, offering solace and guidance. These are mysteries that cannot be proven; they are not measurable, or evidence-based, and I make no pretense of knowing what is true. But I do know the energy and voice of my husband, and right now I feel the presence of the man I was with for almost half my life guiding and scolding me, coming to help me. I decide to trust what I am hearing and allow myself to be led by him. *At least this way, I'll avoid an argument.*

I listen to John's instructions and do not stop until I reach the Ennis Lions Park.

Really? I think. *The local park?*

Stunned that I have driven miles through a raging storm to return to a park less than a mile from where I started, I pull into the parking lot. Mercifully, no one is here. And no fishermen are on the river because the storm is still moving and changing, making it too dangerous to be on the water.

The park has a Little League baseball diamond, and although it's deserted, I can almost hear the cheers and boos of the parents from the well-worn stands. *Perfect*, I think. John loved baseball and was engaged with Ben when he played, spending hours working on the field at the local youth baseball league's diamond. No wonder he got me here: two of his favorite pastimes are represented in this park.

John lets me know that he has directed me to this location. It's as if I'm in conversation with him now. He's telling me it is right for him to be in a place where Ben will know where to find him, where he can bring his own children to see a grandfather they never knew. Unlike the hidden and changeable roadside river locations, Ennis Lions Park, maintained by human beings, will likely survive until such a time as nature's forces reclaim it, as is the eventual way of all things. But what will remain is the place of a ritual grave long blown away by wind and water, a place where Ben can show his children, perhaps even his own son—John's grandchildren—where their grandfather's ashes were given flight, brought there with a promise made by their grandmother.

Walking out of the main part of the park, I stumble off the path and down an uneven patch of ground until I can go no further. I sit on the spongy ground beside the dark waters of the Madison River as the storm front gathers and builds in the sky above me. Facing the craggy, purple-hued mountains that loom over the valley, I watch as the light from the now-dimming sun casts an alpenglow on their peaks, reddish-orange hues fading to grays as the clouds thunder into one another and once again the darkness approaches. The wind begins to scream through the trees, shredding the shuddering bushes surrounding me, whipping the water of the river into oceanic waves. Freezing, I put on every stitch of clothing I've brought with me.

I watch the light leave the edifices of the commanding mountains; it is slowly replaced by a darkness the color of midnight. Everything around me is crying as the clouds cover the sun and the heavens surrender to blackness and I become part of the storm.

A screaming sound arises from the bushes behind me: the vicious winds have blown a baby song sparrow from its nest. The tiny brown-and-black-feathered infant seems to be on the ground somewhere. The shockingly shrill sound of its terror jars me into the present moment, and I try to find the small creature, thinking I might help it back to its nest. It's somewhere behind me in a tangle of sharp brambles and branches. *Oh my God*, I think, *I can't deal with another death*. I can't stand the thought of this little bird separated from its mother, its siblings, alone and terrified. *No more loss*, I cry inside of myself, *no more*. I can't stand by, helpless like I was when John died. I have to rescue this little creature.

The air grows colder, and I wrap myself tighter in my jacket to keep warm as I struggle to find the baby bird. I can barely make it out in the mess of bushes when a louder scream interrupts my search, announcing the arrival of the mother—who, naturally, sees me as an enemy. She screeches both at me and her baby as she prods the little fledging to safety and they both disappear, or at least hunker down together, and become quiet for their own protection.

Wind blows river water into my face, and I too hunker down while the squall continues.

I sit through the storm, clutching the bag of ashes to my chest, feeling unable to move, not wanting to go through with this memorial. Time seems frozen; I am in the deep ambivalence of loss and letting go. I tell myself, *This isn't going to get easier; you're waiting for a "right moment" that will never come.*

Listening now to my own voice, I open the bag of ashes, knowing I need to let them be taken by the wind and the river. I hold them in my open hands and witness their flight away from me—into the air, sinking into the river, scattering on the fecund earth beneath me. I want to close my hands, to keep them with me forever, to keep him with me forever, but I make myself hold my palms open as the cold gusts of wind take the ashes beyond my reach, far away from all that is earthbound and human. Some of the ashes blow back into my face and into my weeping mouth, and I begin to lose track of myself as I sit in this Madison River graveyard. Is that the wailing of the wind, or are the sounds coming from an animal place within me? My lament becomes one with the howling wind, the screaming baby bird—my weeping is a primal growl. My grief becomes the world, the world my grief, as I wail from inside the mouth of the storm surrounding me.

I am sitting in the ashes, shaking and shivering as the cold moves deeper into me. I cannot get up, cannot seem to leave this place. I cannot imagine leaving him here, all alone. I want to lie down and stay here. I feel like I could become wild and never return from that place of wilderness. It's only by a fine thread that I haul myself up, that I know it is not my time, that I must walk away.

Stiff and sore, I struggle to get up and have to crawl a few feet before I find a strong-enough branch to support my standing. I turn my back on the ashes to walk away from the spot. It seems sacrilegious to walk over them, so I try another direction, only to discover that my path is blocked by a fence marking the end of land, making it impossible to exit that way. I can't simply turn my back and walk away. I will have to go over my husband's remains again. I want this to end, but there's something symbolic happening here in my being forced to face the reality of John's death again and again. I have to surrender to the will of the wind, the river, the storms arriving with an unpre-dictable fierceness and leaving with a startling suddenness, stunning me with the power of all that I cannot control. I am carried by these winds that have blown me along and changed me forever.

Stumbling back over John's ashes, I grapple once again with leaving. I purposely don't allow myself to hesitate, however, because my crazed mind somehow believes that if I linger, I will never be able to go.

As I make my way back the way that I came, the sun begins to break through the clouds and the winds start to die down. This whole day has vacillated between harsh winds and rain unpredictably interrupted by a savage, burning sun. As the day moves into evening, the sun has, at least for now, won the battle. Though it is low in the sky, it warms the coldness and ends the darkness with its fading but forceful light.

Emerging from the uneven, hidden path, I reenter the deserted park. The empty baseball diamond sparkles with the remnants of raindrops, and I imagine kids tossing a ball from base to base. Bare picnic tables await birthday parties to come and barbecues of the future.

I don't pause. I don't belong here. There is no future in this place for me. I have left behind my past and must go. Exhausted and continuing to struggle with leaving, I sit in my car in the empty parking lot, still the only human being in the park. Resting, trying to gather enough momentum to start the engine as the dusk of the evening grows, I look up to see that I have been joined by a father and his little boy, rods in hand, heading to the river to fish. I stay and watch them until they disappear through the bushes, down to the river, and then, knowing I will never return, I drive away.

CHAPTER 13

For night's swift dragons cut the clouds full fast,
And yonder shines Aurora's harbinger;
At whose approach ghosts, wandering here and there,
Troop home to churchyards.
—William Shakespeare, A Midsummer
    Night's Dream

NOAA's Space Weather Prediction Center said Sunday
that moderate geomagnetic storm conditions have
already been detected today—and any activity after
nightfall could result in auroras visible as far south
as the northern US. The increased chances for auroras
were caused by a coronal mass ejection, which collided
with Earth earlier today. Coronal mass ejections are
defined by the SWPC as "huge explosions of magnetic
field and plasma from the sun's corona."
—National Weather Service, July 14, 2017

I am fortunate enough to have witnessed the grandeur of
the northern lights twice in my life: once in 1988, when
John and I were drinking and dancing in a cowboy bar in

Montana and ran outside with all the other shit kickers to see the aurora borealis, and now, twenty-nine years later—tonight, July 16, 2017—the night of the day I scattered John's ashes by the Madison River in Montana.

Aurora borealis, named for the Roman goddess of the dawn, Aurora, and the Greek north-wind god, Boreas, is a rare and stunning night-sky phenomenon that's long been the stuff of myths and legends, inspiring stories among North American aboriginal people, who must have looked up into total darkness—unmarred by the presence of the ambient light that exists in our modern world—and watched in wonder as what appeared to be a fire ignited in the sky. From these sky flames, they created stories of warriors and dragons and beliefs in celestial messages both of good will and its dark mirror, evil. Some Inuit tribes believe the lights are the dancing souls of our ancestors. Do the ancestors who have gone before us return as this fiery light to guide us across the boundary of our known world to join them when it's time to travel to the other side? What story is illuminated in the sky tonight in Montana?

Since I scattered John's ashes and drove the mile or two back to Rainbow Valley Lodge from Ennis Park, the treacherous weather of the day has again transformed into a vivid heat. As the dusk turns into night, I sit, exhausted, on the rustic, western-style bench on the porch outside my room, drinking a glass of wine. The other guests are also out, drinking whiskey, laughing, and lying about the size of the fish they caught today—or maybe they're lamenting the fact that they spent too little time on the Madison this afternoon due to the fierceness of the storms. From my rough-hewn perch, I silently observe the sights and sounds of the fishermen laughing and talking while images of my day appear and disappear in my mind's eye. The experiences arise and disappear like mirages that will grow into memories as time passes, and I am content merely to be with them in the dusky shadows of evening's arrival.

It is my last night. I will be leaving Montana tomorrow, and I have no energy to engage in cocktail conversation after the heartbreaking journey of the day. I sit quietly, eating cheese and crackers off a paper towel, munching on an apple, sipping a celebratory chardonnay out of a plastic cup, watching the sky darken.

As the evening grows later and I continue to gaze into space, I notice a glowing vermillion light in the distance. Coming from California, my first fearful thought is that there is a fire coming our way. Glancing toward the road that runs by the lodge, I anxiously strategize my escape route. But fairly quickly, the light begins to spread over the sky above me, moving across the heavens, revealing itself as the emergence of an otherworldly glow.

Chartreuse green and Day-Glo yellow swirls, strips of glittery gold light, all flare across the night sky. Like a kaleidoscope, the colors change as they spiral and spin high above me. By now, the other guests at the lodge have left their rooms. They're getting up from their porch benches, and they're scattering out into the open spaces to look upward. Even Ed comes out of the office to take a look. The immenseness of it all is breathtaking; the colors swirl and shimmer far above us, the sky metamorphosing as sparks of coral appear and disappear in bold stripes, wildly joining the dance of an intense chroma. All of us stand separately, yet we are joined together by a silent sense of wonder.

People start to exclaim.

We are witnessing the arrival of the aurora borealis, and I believe that none of us, so far away from our everyday lives, can truly fathom the privilege of the spectacular nighttime show we are watching unfurl above us.

I notice a group of men heading to the field behind the lodge to get a clearer view, and I decide to join them for the electric panorama. As I walk out over the grassy field, I see that I am the only woman standing among a group of men. I join them, resting my elbows on the fence posts of the pasture. I try to photograph the aurora with my cell phone camera, but it cannot capture the enormity and I give up, decide to simply be present and photograph the images with my mind's eye—to commit what I see to memory within myself.

A more-than-slightly inebriated man stands next to me and excitedly blurts out comments about the magnificent sight we are witnessing. Although he is talking to himself more than he is to me, I respond to his excitement with my own comments. Words, like the photos, are unable to record these images.

The storms of the day have created this spectacular nighttime show of the aurora borealis. The tempest I have traveled through all day has broken the sky open into this phantasmagoric show of light and color. I will learn later that the violent, unpredictable squalls I was making my way through today were caused by an explosion from the sun's corona hitting the earth, that my odyssey through rain and wind today was born out of the shocking arrival of fragments of the sun's plasma infiltrating the planet's atmosphere. Beyond the scientific facts, the world of hard, cold evidence, I think of the Inuit people searching the incandescent heavens for the dancing souls of those who have traveled to the other world and contemplate how earlier today I heard John's words guiding me through the maelstrom to his burial ground.

Looking up into the darkening sky, I am grateful.

CHAPTER 14

*The water you touch in a river is the last
of that which has passed, and the first of that
which is coming; thus it is with time.*
—LEONARDO DA VINCI

The trout fishing season in Montana typically runs from March through November, weather permitting. But the time from mid-June through July offers a three- to four-week window of what is known as magical fishing on the rivers of Montana. Today, I depart Ennis and the Madison River, where I have left John's ashes, little bits of bone that over time will weather and disappear. My time here is over; it went by so quickly . . . as time always does.

It's midmorning, and Rainbow Valley Lodge is quiet, empty of the gregarious fishermen who spend their evenings spinning tales on their porches. By early morning, they're long gone, already floating out on the Madison, wading small streams, crawling along the banks of tiny creeks so as not to spook the catch of the day.

Slowly, reluctantly, I pack the car for my trip back to the Bozeman airport and the return home. This day has dawned with a cloudless, vibrant blue Montana sky, the storms of yesterday passing into memories. Time, like a river, twists, turns, and forks and becomes transformed into new waters, flowing from its source to the sea. In my time here, I have transformed into a time traveler, living in a parallel reality between what can be seen and what, by its very nature, remains unseen.

Stopping by the office, I thank Ed once again for his generous gift of a stay at Rainbow Valley Lodge.

"Oh, you are most welcome, Cheryl," he says softly.

I've grown quite fond of this gentle giant of a man.

"You have no idea of how much this trip has meant to me." I consider sharing something more, but I decide that my story is not yet ready to be spoken.

"I hope you will come back and visit us again," he says, and I feel the genuineness of his invitation.

"Well, you never know," I lie.

Ed comes from behind the desk and gives me a warm hug, and then I return to the car and begin my drive out of town.

I have an eerie, empty feeling as I approach Ennis Lions Park, knowing I'm about to leave this place. *How can I leave him here? Who will take care of him?* The urge to pull into the park intensifies, but I fight the impulse, the thought infiltrating that if I return to the banks of the Madison River in Ennis Park now, I will lie down and never leave. It's only now that I understand that I have left a part of me here. Though I know I will never return, I have left my indelible heartprint in this place. In yesterday's ceremony, I left my marriage on the ground and in these waters. I feel a certain agony in this final parting.

The road is empty, which allows me to slow as I approach the park and look out to the right at the winding Madison

River. Standing alone in the river, a fisherman is casting his line in the spot where I placed John. For a brief moment, I see him there, alive again and fishing. Then my vision fades back into reality, and I find myself smiling at the figure fishing in the ashy waters, hoping he's having a good day on the river.

Driving on into my new life, I know I have kept my promise: I have left John where he belongs.

Part II

*If you listen carefully, at the end
you'll be someone else.*

—Mahabharata

CHAPTER 15

It's a funny thing coming home. Nothing changes.
Everything looks the same, feels the same, even smells
the same. You realize what's changed is you.
—F. SCOTT FITZGERALD

Dropping my car in the lot in front of the Bozeman airport, I look about for someone who will check it back in. There are no attendants in this small outdoor parking lot, no one is standing by to check out the car, there are no forms to turn over. I simply find a space, park the rental car, and then head into the airport, all the while looking over my shoulder, expecting someone to track me down and angrily confront me for ditching the car without any official checkout. But then I remember that I am in cowboy country, where the land, the people, and the rules come from a Wild West history that still permeates this part of the world. I've actually liked this wrangling attitude, as it relates to some inherent cowgirl wanderer who's always lived within me—one that only rarely emerges in the day-to-day world of my sometimes-overly-responsible life.

Following this wild and crazy instinctual self, I sit in the bar and, throwing all caution to the wind, finish off my trip with that local specialty, the bison burger, and a local craft beer. My first bite invites guilt-filled images of those giant beasts in Yellowstone Park, but that doesn't stop me from stuffing the delicious meat into my mouth. Gazing out the floor-to-ceiling windows at the mountains of Montana, I take in the big skies before I board the plane and head back to my life in urban Northern California.

As the plane takes off and rises into that Big Sky blue, ascending through giant, milky clouds, I look down at where I have traveled for the past week. The terrain grows distant below me as we fly higher and higher above the land only days ago foreign to me. I watch the winding, midnight blue waters of the Madison River twist away from my sight, turn around a bend, and then disappear as I fly away.

Hours later, descending over the vast river of light that shines up from cities and freeways, I arrive in Oakland, California, the airport of my many departures and returns.

Pre-9/11, John would always be right at the arrival gate to greet me as I made my way off the plane. Upon each arrival, I'd spot him waiting for me with a single red rose. In the time following that day in 2001, I'd deplane and walk down the long, noisy, smelly, often crowded, and slightly travel-worn corridor toward baggage claim, where I would find him waiting, a smile on his face, a rose in his hand. Now, I pass alone through the exit where other passengers are met with hugs and smiles. No one is here to meet me. My chest tightens and my eyes sting as I pass through this hellish exit portal, my breathing jagged. I move quickly toward the baggage carousel that's beginning to rotate, tossing bags for collection, and, after making sure I have grabbed the right generic black suitcase, I walk out into the darkening evening light and my life.

CHAPTER 16

As water filled my eyes,
I sang a song in honor of the dead.
They came for me . . .
The sun, awakened from its dream,
Rose suddenly. I watched it as I died,
And felt the heaviness of all its gold . . .
—Rafael Campo

In fall 2018, a year and a half after returning from Montana, I gather photos, sugar skulls, bones, and other mementos for my Día de los Muertos altar that's become a tradition over the past several decades. Each year, I celebrate the Day of the Dead by honoring all of those who have died, who have crossed over into other worlds. Times passes on, as it does, and with each year there are more photos and mementos to lovingly place on the altar. The spirits of those who have traveled to the other side are invited to return, lured by favorite treats and a bottle of whiskey (a drink once heartily enjoyed by many of those represented in the tableau of the dead). I imagine them feeling enticed to cross through the veil between the living and the dead. Black candles burn to light the way for the dead on their journey from these unseen realms to visit those of us left behind, still bound to the earth.

I continue creating the altar. In one photo, my mother and father stand together, grinning at the camera and holding a sunflower as they stand in front of an old copper-hooded brick fireplace in a home whose cottage walls, long ago knocked down, have been replaced by a gaudy, brownish-orangish stuccoed two-story mansion overlooking the ocean. My mentor, my teacher, dead nine years now, is still present with me; at times, it seems he's just over my shoulder in my psychotherapy office. As I stand in front of the altar, he looks on from his perch on the mantle. His kind but always-searing gaze, burning with uncomfortable questions and keen insights, follows me around the room. Gently, carefully, I place photos of two young cousins, tragically gone—one from mental illness, the other from an overdose that took him too young—next to each other. Drugs and alcohol being contributing factors in both deaths, in a fit of dark humor, I question their seating arrangement—directly next to the whiskey—on the altar.

Such are the inner conversations within me as I hold each photograph in my hands, looking at faces and places once so familiar, now distant memories. Grandparents, friends, and my first love, taken early by ALS, line up next to one another, a collage of the troubled and beloved departed. Callie, my faithful dog, who had to be put down a month after John died, sits forever beautiful beside Lucy the cat, my familiar—the two joined together in death as they most certainly would never have been in life.

I sit with these souls who have traveled on, remembering stories, images of moments spent laughing, crying, and screaming, times that will never come again but that live deeply within me. This evening, I laugh, cry, occasionally scream, alone. I tell my dead loved ones stories of my life, of what has occurred for me since they left. I think that my critical mother would be pleased with me, and that my sensitive and troubled father, who always wanted to write a book himself, would be proud of my two published books. Night falls; it is a silent and respectful ritual.

John in his baseball cap, smiling and waving at the last game his son pitched, looks out onto the room, and his eyes seem to find mine as I light each candle and sit in front of all those who are no longer here. In the months since scattering his ashes that violent, stormy day in Montana, I have felt his presence fade, and I imagine him flying about in some universe or other as he explores a territory that I cannot enter. His photo goes in the center of the altar, and I place my hand over his waving one, as if a touch, a word, a plea for contact might actually draw him back. I do not linger too long, however, as the ache in my heart begins to crack open into a gaping hole.

I move between gratitude for the time we had together and a strong, surreal disbelief that John is actually on an altar for the dead and not in the next room in our home. Día de los Muertos is a celebration of those who have died, a colorful festival that sends encouraging missives to departed spirits for the success of their journeys. It holds both mourning and celebration of those who have died, but I feel no celebration in John's passing, only a mournful emptiness that longs for his return . . . and again this strange sense of unreality overcomes me. Will that ever change?

I wonder.

Two years after John died, less than a year after my trip to the Madison River, my friends Bill and Shash gave me a gift: a personal mythology created for me by a Celtic story-teller. The myth chosen for me was the story of Mis, who, while little is written about her, is known as the original wild woman of Irish mythology.

Mis was the daughter of Dáire Dóidgheal, a powerful ruler from Europe who set out to invade Ireland. A fierce battle raged for a year and a day until Dáire was eventually slain, which brought the battle to an end. In the days that followed, Mis came to search the bloody battlefield, looking for her father. Upon finding his dead, bleeding body, she became overwhelmed with grief. Casting herself over his mortally wounded body, she began to lick and suck at his wounds like a wild animal trying to heal him. Unable to bring him back from the dead, a madness came over her, and she rose up into the air and flew away into the heart of the Sliabh Mis mountains.

Mis lived in the mountains for many years. Over time, she grew long, trailing fur and feathers to cover her naked skin, and great, sharp claws that she used to attack and tear to pieces any creature or person she met. She could run like the wind, and no living thing was safe from her. She was believed to be dangerous, and all feared the wildness of her grief.

It came to pass that the king in those parts, Feidlimid Mac Crimthainn, offered a reward to anyone who would capture Mis alive. For fear of her, no one accepted except for one man, a gentle harper by the name of Dubh Ruis. Dubh Ruis was able to entice Mis out of hiding and make love to her. He coaxed her into a pool and, over a period of days, washed away the dirt and scrubbed away her feathers and fur. He combed her hair, fed her, and made a bed for her. Eventually, he brought her back to civilization and married her, and Mis then lived a long, full life.

Mis is the archetypal madwoman who lives within each of us. She screams the rage we are afraid to express, she wails the grief that threatens to swallow us whole, she expresses the unacceptable inner voices we suppress out of fear. At the heart of Mis's story is the need to honor mourning in all its wild expression of rage and grief so that one can once again open a broken heart to love. In Ireland, this expression of mourning is called Caoine, something the rest of us might know as keening or funereal dirges. These primal mourning songs date back to the Etruscans and the wakes held by the ancient Greeks. They briefly join the mourner with the departed in the liminal space between life and death; through keening, the mourner can let go of the grief and return to daily life.

Returning from the wildness of Montana and the Madison River memorial, I was called back from the underworld to reenter the upper world of my day-to-day life. I was living in two worlds, one an urban scene of responsibilities and schedules, the other an inner wilderness that flowed constantly beneath my feet like a river as I walked through each day and night. Disorienting and unpredictable, it was exhausting work to keep track of myself as I simultaneously struggled with a sense of unreality and negotiated my life as a responsible human being residing in the world of the living. No one really knew the depth of my struggles—living in the land of the dead even as I paid taxes, laughed at parties, and then drove home alone in the dark. Somehow I managed to continue my daily existence even as, like Mis, I wailed and raged in an imaginary mountain cave.

CHAPTER 17

You can decorate absence however you want—
but you're still gonna feel what's missing.
—Siobhan Vivian, *Same Difference*

Día de los Muertos allows us time for reflection on that which was once our present and now has become our past. The memory is kind to those of us who are fortunate to grow older. Our images, in losing their sharpness, become softer as time passes. Building an altar to the dead carries us to treasured memories and forgotten lands, unexpected moments we may have forgotten. Such is the nature of remembrance . . .

On this November 1, 2018, I pause to gather myself and take a break by sitting for a while in front of the altar in progress. My gaze travels around the room. The stunning modern painting on the wall—given as exchange for psychotherapy when such things were allowed—revives in me thoughts of the artist, who grew from making tiny drawings to creating large installations in nature. The colorful tribe of John's elephant collection has now been relegated to other shelves to make room for the Día de los Muertos altar. My eyes land on the top of the bookshelf, where, proudly displayed, are the two books that I have written. The second one launched a year after my return from Montana in July 2017—now three months ago, in August 2018. I held the launch in San Francisco.

Picking up my well-worn first copy, I find myself back at that gathering.

Standing in front of the groups of people at the events organized to celebrate the publication of my books, I am always aware of a seat left empty by John's absence. Smiling faces look up at me, the eyes of those I know filled with loving encouragement. Even strangers exude kindness. Tonight, a skeptical-looking man at the back of the room, eyes narrowed, looks ready to pounce on my thoughts, the words I have written. *Well,* I think to myself, *there's always a least one contrarian in the crowd with a challenging viewpoint.* But I feel a flutter of anxiety scampering across my chest, creating a slight havoc in my throat. Is this guy going to be the one to out me for my lack of a PhD or an MD? But he only glares and says nothing throughout the evening. And then I look out and see Ben, who has made it up from Los Angeles for this event, and the room feels full and friendly. But then, as happens on every occasion now, the room goes back to feeling incomplete, and I am momentarily filled with a longing to look out and see John.

"I see you talking to groups of people," John said to me thirty years ago.

"What I am saying? What the hell do I have to say?" I answered back.

This dialogue continued, and it became somewhat clearer after my cancer diagnosis, which is what prompted the writing of my two books. He was alive to learn of the publishing contract for both books and, as always, supported my work, even when it meant hours and days of unavailability. He even suggested and arranged for short writer's retreats for me. He gave me the great gift of loving me as a powerful woman, and of reminding me of that power when I was discouraged and struggling with my own sense of worth. I count how he made me feel confident about myself as one of the deepest losses of his death. I keep waiting for the moment when I will no longer feel the emptiness of his absence at important moments, but so far it hasn't gotten easier.

I think there's an expectation that loss gets easier with time, but I find that the feelings just change and then show up in surprising ways—like in these moments, when someone you love should be present at an important life event and instead you're reminded that they are gone forever.

John will not be present at book readings, birthdays, anniversaries. His daily presence, his smell, the feel of his skin, the sound of his voice, and the times of laughing together are all just memories now.

Piece by piece, moment to moment, John fades away and then, when least expected, a fly-fishing magazine will be delivered, an announcement for an event will show up, a Christmas card will arrive addressed to Mr. and Mrs. John Leonard, and I have to contend with what happened all over again. These continual reminders of the vacant chair feel like the sickness of being in a small boat on roiling waters as a blustery storm buffets me about.

"You'd miss me if I weren't here," I'd joke after doing something that would annoy John.

"I don't know what I'd do," he'd say with a sigh.

Now I say to myself as I look at the empty chair in the audience, *No, it's me who doesn't know what to do. But I'm learning.*

How strange that after his death, I would become the person he saw me being all along.

Putting my book back in its place on the bookshelf, I return to the creation of the altar.

CHAPTER 18

I hear the howl of the wind that brings the
long drear storm on its heavy wings.
—WILLIAM C. BRYANT

B lack feathers are scattered on the Día de los Muertos
altar, symbolizing the wings of death that carry our
departed loved ones between the world of the living and
the vast, unknown territory of the dead. On the two days
of Día de los Muertos, it is thought that those of us left
behind may actually be carried close to the other world on
these black wings—while, of course, not daring to cross all
the way over into the realm of the dead, where we do not
yet belong.

I touch each soft, raven-black feather before placing
them among the photos and mementos of those who are
no longer in the visible, so-called real world. The winged
remains of a bird, once alive but now no longer in flight,
grace the presence of those who inhabit all that we can no
longer touch or see. Stroking the soft blackness of a feather,
I travel back in time to a stormy winter day six months
after John died.

It's the first winter without John, and the rains have returned, and at times I do not know if I am not rain itself. Torrential wind and rain are bashing the branches into my windows; leaves and twigs breaking off of bare branches create small tornados in the maelstrom. I'm having a bad day.

My chest feels shredded, and I'm actually gasping for air, my breath rattling, choking on sobs. I wander from room to room, unable to be still, incapable of being soothed. I feel rudderless, again lost in the middle of the ocean with no land in sight. Then I find myself in my kitchen, standing over the sink, witnessing the squall, looking out at the small hummingbird feeder, empty of its sugary, scarlet treat. The cobwebs that have wrapped around the feeder are blowing wildly, and yet, amazingly, they stay attached to the neglected feeder. It was John's job to take care of the hummingbirds.

Suddenly, a hummingbird appears at the window next to the feeder. Its small wings beat furiously against the gushes of water battering its tiny body; it stays in place right in front of me and does not fly off. While I admit to being prone to anthropomorphizing, this small creature and I are in fact in a staredown, and I imagine he is angrily confronting me for my lack of attention to his needs. His red and green markings have given me his gender. I know the females, for protection from predators, are brown or gray—better for blending in.

I begin to sob as he glares at me, unrelenting in his attention. He clearly could care less about my emotional state; he is in a fight for his survival. *I have to take care of him*, I think. I have to take over the job of providing for the hummingbird community that has relied on John to feed them, particularly during the sparseness of the winter months. *This small creature is depending on me*, I say to myself, and I begin to bundle up to head outside.

Still crying, I head out into the storm, into the backyard, to fetch the ladder needed to reach the feeder. While it's not too heavy, it's bulky, and the metal is cold and slippery as I leverage its weight and clumsiness to carry it to the front window. I make my way through the downpour, clanking against the side of the house, the cold metal banging my knees and hips.

After setting the ladder as securely as possible, I climb up the slippery rungs to reach the feeder.

The hummingbird—this small yet powerfully determined creature who's challenged me to come out of my own despair, to move beyond my own boundaries and remember that there are others depending upon me, to become his guardian—watches me fiercely as I struggle in the storm. This bird defies me to fight the strong, dark force of my pull to collapse, all the while reminding me of the force of nature, of all we cannot control, of what we can do in the face of what is beyond our power to change.

After filling the hummingbird feeder, I inch back up the ladder and reach out to rehang it on its hook. My feet are sliding on the wetness of the metal ladder, and I'm afraid that the spongy ground I've planted the ladder in won't hold steady. I quickly and firmly wipe away images of myself crashing to the concrete below me in some tangled mess.

Carefully, yet with more power than I have felt in a long time, I make my way back down the ladder and carry it back to the yard. As I go back inside, I realize that I am drenched. But I've made it! I feel proud of having conquered my fears and faced another storm.

Once the coast is clear, the hummingbird returns to feed. We've made peace with each other, and I have accepted that I am now the caretaker of him and his community. I feel a sense of gratitude to this delicate creature who has literally gotten in my face and forced me to take action. "Yes," I say to him as his beating wings stop for a moment and he teeters on the edge of the feeder to take in its nourishment again, "I will take care of you. John is gone. But I'm here."

It will be another six months before I go to Montana. In this moment, I can't begin to imagine how many months it will take before I'll feel like I can stand fully on my own without John.

As I return from my storm-tossed reverie, I remember the terrified squeals of another tiny bird, battered and tossed from its nest during the violent storm by the Madison River when I scattered John's ashes, and I wonder how it has fared over the long Montana winter. Who has watched over that small creature who lives in a wild land with no bereft widow to care for him?

When I lay the final jet-black feather on the altar, I realize that in the nearly two years since I made the commitment to be the new hummingbird guardian, I have clambered up the ladder in the heat of summer and endured the shaky climb in the chill of another passing winter. The feeder has never again gone empty. The familiar routine of my little caretaking system is strangely comforting as I continue to struggle with rebuilding my life. In an inner world so full of sorrow and uncertainty, these are small triumphs of healing; these are the wings that carry us until we find a place to land.

CHAPTER 19

My biggest worry is that when I'm dead
and gone, my wife will sell my fishing gear
for what I said I paid for it.
—HAS BEEN ATTRIBUTED TO BOTH KOOS BRANDT
AND TONY WARELIUS

In the ritual tradition of Día de los Muertos, the spirits of those who have died are sometimes convinced to circle back to us during the two days at the beginning of November if we put some of their favorite things on the altar. Desperately wanting John to swing by, if only for a brief visit, I figure I'll put something from his vast collection of fly-fishing equipment up there. I get up from my seat in front of the altar and bravely venture into the frighteningly cluttered space I call a garage, home to John's collection of "vital" fly-fishing paraphernalia, and look for a memento to place on the 2018 altar.

I look at the treasure trove of rods, some handmade by John—now kept in a space far away from a trout stream, put away, never again to be handled by their master, their maker. Left behind and alone, they remain dry and unused in their cases. I can't bear to look at them. Nor can I completely turn my back on them.

Two years ago, the tension of this ambivalence froze me from taking any action, but my frozen state thawed a bit when I decided that I would give some of John's rods to friends, two men whose love of fishing connected them to John, men who had fished alongside him.

Several months after John's death, Bill and Shash came to visit, and it seemed like a good opportunity to let Bill pick a rod for himself. I wandered out to the garage with him and watched his slightly veiled horror as he took in the quasi-hoarder scene before him. The whole area the rods were in was in a chaotic, disorganized state, and I showed him the mess, telling him to pick one he wanted. I was happy that he'd fish with it, I told him; it would make me feel good.

Bill surveyed the scene quietly, and, because he's not a particularly quiet man, I could tell he was trying to figure out how to work with me in this jumble of junk. After heaving a sigh, he looked at me, raised his eyebrows, and widened his eyes. As we stared at each other, we began to giggle like when we were kids and just a look between us could result in hysterics.

"Cheryl," he said. "I'm a Virgo. I can't be in this space without tidying it up."

"No problem!" I chuckled. "You know I'm always thrilled when anyone is willing to do housework of any kind for me. I mean, really, a tidy garage is a sign of a wasted life."

As Bill began to sort through the rods, the reels, all the fly-fishing equipment that John made, that he fished with,

I began to feel unsettled, anxious. I didn't want to see these rods all lined up next to one another, leaning against a closet in the garage, unused for months, neglected, some of them dusty. I could see John's slender, artistic hands holding these rods, attaching the reels and stringing the line that would later fly out over the stream, sending a small fly in the air to capture a trout. I was standing close to him as he rigged up my reel, readying me to cast my line over the water we were standing in together. My heart pounded and I shook as movies of memory played in my mind.

His back to me, Bill was furiously digging away and organizing the rods and reels. I started cracking jokes, all the while feeling a strange combination of numbness and fear.

"Oh, look," I cried, "that's the rod John made for me." It was a lovely, light rod on which he painstakingly wrote my name in cursive letters after finishing it in a lush burgundy color.

Trying not to show my distress, I said in a muted voice, "I'll keep the rods he made for me. I can't give those away, and I might fish with them again." I felt dizzy and nauseous; my throat tightened, and I wanted to run out of the garage.

Bill looked at me kindly and gently handed me the rod John had made for me.

I held my custom-made rod, flexing it slightly. Muscle memory took over, and I was casting into a pristine mountain stream. I was standing in the front of a small boat on a larger river. I was scanning the riffles in fast-moving water; I was casting my line toward eddies, alongside logs, and up against the edges of dark boulders. "Strike, strike!" John yelled out. And yet again I'd missed another fish. I was standing in the Little Truckee River, the sun beginning to bring warmth to the cold of the early morning. And, finally, I was reeling in a large steelhead, soaked to the bone, standing in the pouring rain, as the day's winter light faded into a gray evening on the lower Sacramento River.

Bill and I were silent as he continued his endeavors and I spun off into reverie. But he is a sensitive man, perceptive, and a keen observer of humans. Bill is no one's, and never has been anyone's, fool. Looking through John's collection, he broke the silence: "I don't know if I can take one." His own discomfort was showing now. "Is it really okay?"

I wondered what he was feeling but couldn't quite muster the strength to ask, to open up the depth of emotions swirling about in the disordered chaos of the garage. Maybe, beneath the jokes and the stillness, we were both feeling the inner sense of unease ragged emotions can bring. I don't know; I didn't ask him.

But then Bill's words brought me back into the garage, and I said, "Oh, please do. John would want that, and it will help me feel better knowing that these rods are being used by people I know. I really need you to do this."

And so Bill picked a rod and a reel, and he took some flies and other fly-fishing accoutrements. It was the first rod to find a new home.

Not only because he likes order but also because he is kind, by the time we'd exited the garage, Bill had organized the entire stock of rods and reels, and the two of us had even done a bit of recycling to clear the space. Throughout all of this, we laughed and made a strained task as enjoyable as possible.

We went back into the house, and while we were sitting at the table with Shash, Bill showed her his cache, and the throat I had held so tightly closed opened and I burst into tears.

No one said a word. Bill quietly put his hand on my shoulder, and the moment passed.

Several months after Bill chose his rod, the second rod from John's collection to find new hands was picked by Tony, John's high school buddy, a friend of many antics in the past (most of them involving the pursuit of girls and drinking beer). John and Tony's reconnection later in life often involved fishing expeditions.

I opened the treasure trove of fly-fishing gear, and Tony found a rod and reel that suited him. This second go-round of giving away some of John's fishing belongings was slightly less painful, perhaps because it happened after a bit more time had passed. It seemed these garage expeditions would get easier after the first wrenching experience with Bill.

Tony perused the flies and the countless fly-fishing books John collected over the decades of his life as a fly fisherman. It was heartwarming to watch him as he excitedly found a fly-tying guidebook that he had long wanted. It went home with him, of course.

Perhaps, I thought, *I am beginning to let go.*

Spurred on by the unexpected positivity of that second giveaway, in December of 2016, six months after John's death, I decided to go and talk to Leo, the owner of the local fly-fishing store, Fish First, about the possibility of selling some of John's rods. They were, after all, worth a pretty good chunk of dough.

I walked into the store for the first time since John's death. Leo was sitting behind the counter, and when he looked over at me, his face fell. John was well-known in the fishing community, and I'd also frequented Fish First over the years, and it was clear that Leo knew.

He offered gentle, sincere condolences. No, he didn't sell rods, but he knew a local guy who did.

I'd made a mistake going there to ask about selling the rods. I muttered to Leo that I'd keep that in mind. He, another kind fisherman, said, "Let me know when you're ready to sell the rods, and I can connect you with the guy I mentioned."

"Thanks, Leo."

I barely made it out of there and back to my car before falling apart.

Now, almost two years later, on this first evening of Día de los Muertos in 2018, no other fishing gear has been moved from the storage spaces, and the garage has been taken over by forgotten and unnecessary junk once again. I select a couple of flies to place on the altar and come back into the house, leaving the garage a place of watery memories. Small, glimmering insects of prey made up of feathers, beads, hair from wild animals—I carefully lay them down in front of John's picture.

"Please come get them," I say out loud, "please circle back from wherever you are, even for a minute."

I feel deeply grateful for Bill and Tony, who continue to tell me how they think of John when they fish with his rods. Whenever he goes out and catches a fish with John's rod, Tony always sends me a text, sometimes a photo of his success. This is both soothing and heartbreaking. Mostly, I am comforted by his and Bill's thoughts and feel a bittersweet happiness that these rods are still out on a stream, being used and appreciated. John would like that.

It is often said that a human being is remembered until the last time someone speaks his or her name. We are ephemeral creatures alighting briefly on earth, all of us careening in the same direction. We leave behind all that we once were and become—what? Air? Sky? Stars? Do our souls, the essence of our being, travel in swirling patterns of light and color in corners of the universe we cannot comprehend, only to circle back and touch others lightly in the heart?

The objects we once held are passed around to others and eventually find themselves in the hands of those with no knowledge of us. Like a fine Stradivarius violin played over centuries by a virtuoso, a good fishing rod, one that is built with great care and fished with masterful skill, may by passed from hand to hand for decades, its previous owner sometimes known and sometimes the shadow of a stranger unbeknownst. Surely it conveys to the person casting over new waters some aspect of the person in whose hands it was once held. Some part of each human who has played that violin or each fisherman who has used that rod to play a fish on a stream is alive in the wood, the strings, the fly line.

I'm taken back to the father and his young son strolling down to the bank of the Madison River, rods in hand, heading for the spot where I'd just left John's ashes. One day, will a grandson or granddaughter of Bill's or Tony's cast a line? Or will Ben eventually pick up one of his father's rods and fish a stream with his own child? I imagine someone miles and years away from where I sit in front of this altar feeling the strike of a trout and then the touch

of an invisible hand, guiding the fish to a net. These ram-
bling imaginings make me feel better, as if there is some
kind of infinite connection that transcends time, a fleeting
illusion of immortality that brings a brief and soothing
comfort to the sting of the inevitable losses of mortality.

CHAPTER 20

The loneliest moment in someone's life is
when they are watching their whole world fall apart,
and all they can do is stare blankly.
—F. SCOTT FITZGERALD

Six months after leaving Montana, on a dusky evening in late fall of 2017, as I was closing the drapes on the large windows in my living room, I watched my ninety-year-old neighbor walk alone into her home. A longtime widow who used to walk miles each day, she now ambled carefully and slowly to her front door from the street in front of her house. Gone were the days when I would meet up with her on the walking path, striding back from the grocery store with yet another stolen cart filled with bargains she would tell me about. In earlier times, you could spy a collection of shopping carts on the side of her home. Now, her family came to pick her up; no more long walks around town.

I stood, watching her go into her home and shut the door behind her. Something inside me kept me at the window, staring out as the fading light turned to darkness.

Would that be me? Was I looking at the ghost of my future? A hollow space began to open up within me, threatening to engulf me.

The Latin meaning of *widow* is "void."

CHAPTER 21

How deeply did you learn to let go?
—Buddha

When I pick the picture of John for the 2018 Día de los Muertos altar, I notice that I skip past pictures of him dressed in a suit and tie and am drawn toward the photos of him later in his life, dressed casually in T-shirts and jeans. He was a handsome man, and as I leaf through photos, I remember how stunning he looked when he was dressed formally. As time went on, he grew to hate suits and ties, but he never got rid of the dress clothes he owned. I looked at John in that suit less than a month before he died. Now, it strikes me that I no longer own that suit. I gave all of his formal clothes away.

It was 2017 and fall was just beginning to turn from bright orange and gold into the gray of winter. Figuring it would be easier to cull through his closet than go through the fishing stuff, I decided to donate John's suits, shirts, ties, and jackets to Wardrobe for Opportunity in Oakland, California.

Founded in 1995 to address often overlooked yet critical barriers to finding and retaining employment, Wardrobe for Opportunity has served nearly thirty thousand low income individuals referred there by more than forty partner social service and job training agencies across the San Francisco Bay Area over the years. Founded originally to provide professional clothing for women, Wardrobe for Opportunity has expanded to provide in-depth, 360-degree professional development for men and women. The organization has scheduled times for people to donate clothes at drop-off spots, and the clothes are subsequently made available to people who are working toward employment, often during or after times of great difficulty, including homelessness and mental illness.

Earlier in his life, John lived and worked as a real estate broker in Oakland for many years. This "former life" required business attire and suits, ties, and well-pressed shirts. These outfits had remained in his closet for the occasional wedding, fine dining experience, and funeral. I knew he'd like give back to the community of Oakland by donating some professional outfits for a man who was looking to make some changes in his life. And so, in the spirit of continuing to let go, I decided on a date in the fall after my return from Montana.

I'd taken some of his things to the cleaners, because the man receiving these items deserved clean, well-pressed clothes. The thought of some guy feeling uplifted and ready for an opportunity in his life because of John's clothes gave me a warmhearted feeling. The night before the early morn-ing Saturday delivery at the pick-up spot in downtown

Oakland, I pulled shoes, shirts, and pants out of the closet, set aside hangers, and opened up the ironing board. I plugged in the iron, looked at the piles of his belongings, and began.

When I polished his dress shoes, I placed my hand inside each shoe and felt the imprint of his foot beneath my fingers. I remembered his slender feet warming mine after sliding into a cold bed. I touched the grooves inside the shoe almost as if I could touch the bottom of his foot.

I ironed each shirt with the care of something you do for the last time. There was no preparation of a body for burial; no ritual washing took place in the early hours of May 14, 2016, before John was carried out of the house in a thick, black bag. I began to weep as I now honored his body in the only way I was able, by meticulously ironing each shirt with love. These shirts that touched his chest reminded me of the hour after he died, when he lay so horribly still and grew colder on the floor of the family room of our home, when I lay next to his body, holding him, placing my head on his chest where I had so often rested, when I made otherworldly, keening noises that shattered the eerie quiet after the noise of the emergency crew who had tried to revive an already dead man.

Now, as I touched the cloth, my tears fell into the steam rising up like a fog from the iron. Some cultures spend days with the body of the beloved—bathing it, chanting over it, a reverent cleansing ritual preparing the deceased for the journey to the next world. I had such a short time before John was taken in a black bag and driven to a mortuary less than a mile away. I remembered now how, in my crazed state of crisis, I lamented that he was alone and thought, *I should go, too, so that he won't feel alone.*

Continuing with my preparation of his clothes for donation, I put each one of his jackets on backward, running my hands to the back and down the sleeves, as if he could hold me just one more time. I searched for a lingering scent of him as I buried myself in a jacket. I was dancing with him; I felt the warmth of his body (he always ran a little hot) pressed against mine. In his jacket, I swayed around the room in a hazy, visual last dance of memory.

I took a break because I was wailing now, gasping. I was just present enough to put the hot iron down.

I finished late at night, exhausted with grief.

The next morning, I carefully carried the assortment of clothes and shoes to the car and began my journey to downtown Oakland, a fifteen minute drive from my house. As I traveled each mile, I kept thinking of turning back around and taking it all back to his closet, as if that would somehow ease my ache. It was the beginning of a deeper knowing that an ache sometimes lives within you forever.

Pulling up behind a short line of cars, I stopped and looked out the window from the driver's seat. A rack of clothes stood on the sidewalk, and only one woman was present to take the donations. I imagined telling her the story of John's clothes, of his death. I wanted to tell her how much it would mean to him to know that his stuff was going to help out some guy in Oakland. But she had her system down; this was no time for some wreck of a widow pulling on her and getting in her way.

I inched along until I was first in the queue. I put my car in park, and she and I unloaded the clothes. I watched her hang them on a bulging rack of men's and women's clothes. I tried to hold it together as she cheerfully thanked me, gave me the form to file this donation on my taxes, and turned to the person in the car behind me.

I looked at the donation form in my hand in disbelief and a kind of weird horror that it had all just come down to writing my husband's clothes off my taxes.

I wasn't able to drive away yet. I pulled up beyond the line of cars and watched to make sure nothing happened to John's clothes, that they were not left unattended on a littered, depressing slab of concrete sidewalk. That same bizarre feeling of not wanting to leave him, or even his possessions, alone, of not wanting to abandon him, filled me once again.

Now I was remembering when I left his ashes by the Madison River three months earlier, how I struggled to leave, how I wanted to stay there. I was far from being beside a roaring river surrounded by purplish blue, towering mountains, of course; I was in my car on an urban street shadowed by tall concrete buildings, watching the woman who'd collected John's stuff, keeping an eye on the clothes rack.

I stayed until I saw her wheel the rack into the building. My eyes followed the rack with his clothes, moving out of sight, for always, forever.

Once again, I drove away.

One year later, I gaze up at the altar and realize that the letting go has not gotten easier. How could I have known about the unexpected fissures of my heart that would continue to break me open time and time again? I look up at the photo of my dear friend Diana, dead from melanoma six years, herself a widow and my traveling companion on many wondrous adventures. Out loud, I apologize to her.

"I didn't understand," I tell her. "I'm so sorry. I didn't know what you were going through when Joe died. I would have known how to be with you so much better now that I know what I know. I had no concept of what it's like to lose a life partner. I would have done better. Please forgive me for not understanding the devastating grief of losing Joe."

Her sparkling eyes and wry smile greet me from her preserved image atop a camel in Egypt, a photo taken decades ago. "Oh, now, Cheryl," she'd surely say. "Don't be ridiculous."

I wish she were here with me. We'd agree that the loss of a partner does not get easier and discuss how annoying it is that others expect you to get over it. Like a river meandering along its path, sparkling in the sunlight, beneath the surface, the water is always made of tears.

CHAPTER 22

Until we stop harming all other living beings,
we are still savages.
—THOMAS A. EDISON

In the growing dark and chill of fall, when the dusky shadows of winter begin their foggy descent, I brave the apocalyptic scene in my garage once again to search for items on John's fly-tying bench as a way to commemorate his love of fly-fishing on the Día de los Muertos altar.

On this first day of November, as I enter the mayhem of the garage, for once I actually do know exactly where I need to go to find the accoutrements of the angler—though only because of another hunting expedition that occurred in this same space just months ago.

During the early summer this year, I began to notice growing and disturbing signs of rodents in the garage. At first I just kept cleaning up their poop, deluding myself that the Shop-Vac and copious sprays of Windex would take care of the problem. Positive that I'd destroyed their habitat, I celebrated after I emptied a tiny little abandoned home out of one of my fishing boots. But a day later, when I was still cleaning the tiny black turds off of John's fly-tying bench, I discovered another well-built nest tucked in a corner behind feathers and pieces of yarn. And as I was looking down, a small creature darted off along the shelving right next to me and disappeared from view.

Shuddering, I fled from this looming, furry, seemingly enormous gray fiend who was clearly out to infect me with a deadly strain of bubonic plague.

And so logic prevailed and, after all of these gag-producing failed attempts to rid the garage of infestation, and particularly as the droppings seemed only to multiply hours after I had reigned terror upon the mouse community, I went to my local hardware store to purchase a trap that would catch but not kill the mice so I could release them into the wild, unharmed and free to roam anywhere else but in my garage. This seemed to me to be a variation of catch-and-release fishing, adjusted to the hunt of rodents in my garage.

I tempted my little interlopers with globs of peanut butter at the backs of the traps so as to provide them with a tasty treat prior to their capture. I wondered if they would have chosen peanut butter for their last meal as I sampled some of the delicious organic product I'd purchased to seduce them.

Days into this humane catch-and-release hunting method, however, the peanut butter was solidifying into a concrete mass. With no takers, this method also failed.

Back at the hardware store, I purchased some small devices that were supposed to emit ear-splitting sounds that would drive the tiny creatures from their habitat.

Several days later, I was back to my Shop-Vac-and-Windex plan; I continued to clean up the mess left by these creatures who clearly had seen it all when it came to these instruments of capture—or who were wearing ear plugs to protect themselves from the sound supposedly emanating from the devices strategically placed in the garage.

On my next return to the hardware store, I read the description of how the rodents would die if I used poison. Horrified and feeling guilty, I quickly exited the store without a purchase.

Finally realizing that I would have to resort to murder, I borrowed a small trap that would electrocute the unsuspecting mouse once it ventured within, in search of the small bits of cat food placed at the back of the trap. Battery-operated, a light would flash when there was a successful kill. I renamed the device The Electric Chamber, placed it strategically, turned it on, and exited the garage.

Less than ten minutes later, I peeked back inside. A blinking light told me the news of the capture. Donning thick gloves, I picked up the trap to find a tiny, gray, limp little mouse who, apparently and hopefully, never knew what had hit him. I burst into sobs, crying and blithering to the deceased, tiny being, "I'm sorry, I'm so sorry." I broke down looking at this innocent creature, who was only seeking shelter and a snack to survive, and was filled with horror and shame. I carried the electric torture device to the outdoor garbage can. Sickened, I dumped the mouse into what now would become my mouse graveyard.

After this sad little burial, I sat, covered my face, and cursed this onerous job that I wouldn't have to do if John were here. In my state of guilt and fury, I felt a deepening wrath that I had been forced to take on the duties that would have been John's, and I screamed obscenities into the air. My usually strong filter was ripped and shredded when I tried to absorb the wildness of killing a living creature. I, the woman who carefully wrapped spiders in tissue and carried them outside, who apologized to the ants she had drowned or mass murdered with organic sprays of some orange liquid or trapped in little houses of sweet poison, now found myself dumping a cute little mouse in a trash can. My career as a serial killer had taken off.

That same day, twenty minutes later, I peeked around the corner in the darkened garage and saw the bright red light blinking again. *Oh no*, I thought, *there's more*. Wishing I owned a hazmat suit, I put the thick gloves back on and headed for the little murder box.

Just beyond the entrance of the metal box, a lifeless baby gray mouse was stretched toward the cat food at the back of the trap. No bigger than half my little finger, I imagined it was the child of the mouse I had already killed. With apologies but not quite as upset this time, I buried the creature next to the first victim in the open grave of the garbage can. I felt disgusting.

But then something rather alarming began to happen: as the hours went on, I began to obsessively check the trap. I recognized within me that primal human excitement of the kill. Me, who hated any form of violence, for the first time in my life was feeling the thrill of the hunt, the attraction to a blood sport. I actually began to experience the satisfaction of capture, the power of being the master of my territory. I began to feel an excitement in my success as the destroyer of vermin and was both proud of and appalled by myself.

During my time as a great hunter and destroyer of mice in my garage that summer of 2018, I counted a coup of eight mice in less than twenty-four hours. Each received a moment of atonement, and all were laid to rest together.

Today, when I find the bits and pieces of fly-tying material I'm looking for on John's bench, there are no signs of mice—all is quiet on the Western Front. But as I leave to take the items to the altar, I pause to check the small electric chamber that I have left in the garage, just to be sure.

My killing days are behind me; I feel glad and deeply relieved to spot the unblinking light, the empty trap, the small pieces of cat food still uneaten. I close the door to the garage and return to the altar, thinking of the souls of those little mice. *Should I place something on the altar for them?* I wonder. *Who am I to judge who is worthy of being remembered on Día de los Muertos?*

My Día de los Muertos ritual honors mostly those whom I miss dearly and with whom I would love to have just one more moment. Yet the mice who gave their lives in my garage taught me that I could face a task once taken care of by John, that I was capable of meeting a challenge that horrified me. We can choose to collapse under the weight of our losses, our reluctance to moving forward in our own lives, or we can learn to let go of what we cannot change and of what, or who, is no longer.

I don't believe I will ever feel gratitude for John's death, but as the fall evening darkens into night on this day of Día de los Muertos, I feel grateful to those mice who gave their lives in order for me to find my own courage to carry on. I light a small candle to honor the community of gray mice who once took shelter in the dark recesses of my garage.

CHAPTER 23

The key to a women's heart is an unexpected gift at an unexpected time.
—SEAN CONNERY

The 2018 altar is nearly complete, except for a memento from John's career as a jewelry designer. The backyard chicken coop that served as his studio was remodeled in 2001, and since the spring of 2017 it has stood abandoned. I haven't entered it in over a year, but now I wonder if there may be something in there to add to my altar. So I grab my keys and head out.

Struggling with the thickness of a door that's been locked for over a year, I have to push with my entire body to gain entrance to the studio.

It is now a shell of what was once an alive production space. There's a scent of mold, a smell of disuse that lingers in the air mingling with a feeling of moody emptiness. Large pieces of outdated casting equipment remain lined against the wall, a small kiln ready to receive metal offerings remains open, and bits and pieces of silver and gold shimmer among a jumble of wax models. It gives me a desolate, melancholic feeling when I see the once-active equipment now looking shabby and worn. Scraps of broken creations, pieces that weren't born the way they should have been, are randomly scattered on the bench, still awaiting their fate in the crucible that will melt them once again into a molten flow of metal, ribbons of gold, a river of silver. A friend and fellow jeweler once remarked upon her entrance into the studio after John's death, "Ah, this is the studio of a metalsmith." In that moment, what I had seen as turmoil transformed into a beautiful disarray of artistry.

As I look at the empty spot where John's jewelry bench stood, I recall the day I sold it. I see myself with the young woman, whose work I greatly admire, watching her handling the tools, hearing her asking me for prices.

"How much for the bench?" she asked, looking hopefully at me. She had a small wad of cash with her; the amount she could pay for the bench was far below its worth, and I struggled to hold to my asking price.

"I'm sorry," I mumbled, "I really can't settle for that amount."

Her bright, young, dark eyes met mine, and she said, "I understand. I know it's worth more than I can pay." She did make some other significant purchases, however, and as she handed me the money, she told me what an honor it was to take the tools of another jeweler.

"I like to handle the tools that other hands have used to create beautiful objects. I feel their lineage through my own hands."

We stood together in a moment of gratitude before she departed.

Just weeks later, that same spring, I found a buyer for John's bench. Quite by chance, I met a lovely woman from Los Angeles who was starting her career as a jeweler, and I sent her pictures of the bench and the remaining equipment. She arranged a trip to Northern California, and a date for the sale and delivery of the bench was set.

Early in the morning on the appointed day, I spent hours readying the bench for its new owner.

An ancient music player, formerly known as a boom box, sat on a narrow shelf along with some small shells, pieces of found wood twisted into shapes like creatures, waves—all objects of the designs of nature that John loved. There was a cassette in the tape deck, and I pushed the start button. Pachelbel's Canon in D began to play, and I, with tears streaming down my face, began the ritual cleaning of John's bench.

As I rubbed the grain of the wood, cleaning and polishing the grime away, I felt pride in his work and his capacity to create and adapt instruments and invent contraptions that worked as well as the expensive apparatuses sold at far higher prices because they were labeled as "jeweler's tools." I removed his visors, his masks, held them in my hands, even placed them on my own head. I stripped the bench of the array of jewelry-making paraphernalia whose purpose I had no idea about. Small scraps of paper with unfinished designs—his handwriting, his maker's mark, all that his hands had touched—I moved from the bench. They would stay with me. I cleaned every corner, years of metal dust, my hands pressing into the wood, removing what I could of the scratches, the marks of a metalsmith. Pulling back and observing my work, I looked at a bench that would now move on; more would be created, the hands of another would open its drawers and make new messes, there would be successes and failures. Like the fishing rods that found new fishermen, the bench had found a new designer.

Now I stand in the nearly empty studio one year later, remembering that I have moved the stone collection, the precious metal pieces of gold and silver, and all of the remaining jewelry inventory into John's small home office, and as I exit the studio, a familiar emptiness grows within me, making it hard to breathe. I feel a familiar nausea threatening to overwhelm me, and I swallow the sickness that's beginning to gag me.

Using all my strength, I pull and tug the studio door closed. With one final yank, I shut the entrance to the space and return to the house.

The small office in the house was John's office and design space. I haven't done much to this compact work area. It looks as if someone was there a moment ago and rushed off in a hurry, leaving behind half-completed projects. Sudden death leaves much unfinished in its treacherous wake.

Hidden behind some boxes, I find the ring holder John used when he built a wax model before casting the design into metal. On it is a lovely wax model of a ring with a turquoise stone that is almost finished. In the tumultuous time after his death, I didn't notice this small gift—which, I am certain, was meant for me on my sixty-fifth birthday, which fell two weeks after he died.

I hold in my hand a ring never to be finished, an unexpected gift. I carefully place the wax creation in a small box, but it crumbles as I place it on the tissue. I have destroyed his last design, his sweet gift to me. Devastated, I close the lid to this ring box, containing within it a broken design and a stone the color of the desert sky. I cannot bear to throw it away but also need to keep it out of my view.

My chest aching, the sick feeling still present, my eyes puff up with unshed tears as I continue my search for an object for the altar. Shuffling through the mess of John's office, I sort through some envelopes and find one that seems a bit thicker than the rest of the stack. Upon opening it, I find $560 in cash. I am sure, without a doubt, that this was his "stash" to celebrate my birthday with. It's another unexpected gift. Holding the money in my hands, I can hear him saying to me, "Don't pay bills with this. Take it for yourself; do something frivolous." It's one of those bittersweet moments when I feel how he lives in me. It's what can happen when we listen to a silent language that is spoken from a deep inner reality and hear the phrases, the sound, of a voice we have known intimately. In this way, the dead inhabit our consciousness, giving us "messages from the grave." All we need to do is suspend the rational mind and they're right there, where they've been all along.

Truth is, suspending the rational mind comes naturally to me. Also in truth, this quality of mine used to drive John nuts.

I choose the few tools still left and a small silver trout and leave the office to place them on the altar.

Later, I decide to use this unexpected gift of cash to buy some clothes to wear when I speak and teach. In this way, I'll bring him with me when I face crowds of strangers. I know he's still got my back.

CHAPTER 24

Love is like a virus. It can happen to
anybody at any time.
—MAYA ANGELOU

The Día de los Muertos altar is complete and will remain up for the next three days. My new friend, Dianne, invites me to my first singles Meetup in San Francisco. It's held monthly at the Press Club, a swanky cocktail lounge in a stylish part of the city that caters to the prowling, adventurous elite.

Finished with my altar project, I spend the weekend worrying and wondering if I should go or not. What I should wear? What if no one talks to me? What if someone *does* talk to me? I sit in front of the altar, talking to John's picture and asking for advice—or perhaps I'm really asking for permission. Is it okay to do this? He doesn't offer an opinion one way or another.

And so, after much obsessing, on the morning of the Meetup, I tell myself to "get over it, and just go and have a good time." Looking up at the photograph of John waving at me from the altar, I say out loud, "Oh, all right, I'm gonna go." He remains silent and I, feeling more than slightly insane, find myself hoping that his spirit is feeling jealous. These thoughts and feelings serve to validate my choice to go to this type of event before I am lost forever in this alternative universe in which I travel.

It's a stormy night, an early precursor to a winter that will finally release us from the ravages of the years of drought in Northern California. Rain is slashing down on my car as I drive across the bridge to San Francisco; the roads are slick and drivers are sliding around, unused to driving on rain-soaked roads. Día de los Muertos is in many ways the kickoff of the winter holiday season. This Meetup is a reminder of that, since the event is actually titled "The Jingle Mingle." *Oh my God.*

I survive the perils of the oily, slippery roads and miraculously find the underground parking garage near the Press Club, which is cavernous and nearly empty. I feel nervous about the lack of people in the area and revert back to my old trick of carrying my keys in my hand with one key between each of my fingers, just in case I need to fend off an assault. As I try to figure out how to get out of this subterranean concrete bunker, it occurs to me how completely ridiculous it is to believe that I could actually defend myself with a car key.

I worry that I won't be able to find my way back later, but I try to take note of where I am and what elevator I've just entered to take me up to the street level. Upon emerging aboveground, I stand before the massive edifices of closed museums and chic shops and try to get my bearings.

I'm cold and wet. I fight the urge to just turn around and go home.

Looking around, I notice a subtle, posh, all-glass entrance with a small, tasteful sign barely visible above the doors: Press Club. The long and lean dark-haired beauty of a hostess greets me in her slinky, miniature black dress. Her voice is like a strand of silk gliding over my chilled body, which suddenly seems short and chunky in comparison to the one belonging to this lithe young siren, who is luring the holiday revelers to the underground mingle below.

I can hear the sounds of clinking glasses and cocktail chatter downstairs. *Please don't fall down the stairs*, I plead with myself, as I head down the polished silvery (and slippery) chrome-and-glass staircase to the elegant lounge below. *Stand straight, breathe deep, here we go.*

Light natural wood walls offset the dark, sunken adult playground. Dim and sexy lighting guard against the dangers of anyone not looking absolutely impeccable in the modern lounge, with its stylish and restrained minimalist décor. Massive abstract modern art pieces, subtle splashes of gold, are carefully hung on walls surrounding arrangements of low leather couches and chairs in trendy neutral colors. I've chosen black for the evening and have added my own splash of color with an artsy necklace that I can always count on to get me compliments. I keep my black leather jacket on, and I'm deeply grateful that my fashion choices blend in with the aesthetics of the space.

Looking through the noisy mob, I spot Dianne at the bar, sipping a fine-stemmed glass of rosé. Younger than me by more than a decade, she brings a bright light and a wicked sense of humor to this singles-scene muddle. She's also chosen the seemingly mandatory black clothing, which signals sophistication despite the fact that it is actually an understated attempt to hide vulnerability.

Dianne and I like each other a lot; we beam at each other, each glad to have an ally in what could potentially be a lonely outing.

After our initial clinging behavior, we decide to honor the theme of the evening by mingling. It's been over thirty years since I've done anything like this, and back then I was a thirty-five-year-old woman with long, black, curly hair who was kind of a hot mess. This evening, I fret that I'm a sixty-seven-year-old woman who's just a mess, without the hot factor to fall back on. I look around and consider that I am one of the oldest people at this bar. "Grandma does Meetup," I joke to Dianne. But within minutes, an attractive man approaches us and, following an introduction which actually includes the unbelievable line "Do you come here often?" we all laugh and he launches into a conversation about his ex-girlfriend coming with her new boyfriend which seems slightly odd as this event seems slanted to the singles crowd.

Our new pal, Klaus, is feeling anxious, he admits. It's hard to imagine as I gaze at his handsome, chiseled jaw and startlingly azure eyes. His accent is faintly German, or perhaps Austrian, and he tells us that he was a competitive skier but now, thanks to a knee injury, has a contracting business. Being therapists, Dianne and I are good listeners who know how to ask just the right questions, and soon the three of us have formed a little triad at the bar at the Press Club.

Klaus maintains that he doesn't drink, but as the evening progresses, that appears not to be completely true. Indeed, his accent grows less European and more American as our time together progresses and the wine continues to flow. In spite of it all, he's a remarkably genuine and likeable character, someone Dianne and I will gravitate toward in future gatherings even though he's not a dating prospect. His lovely blond Swiss ex comes over, her new boyfriend's arm wrapped around her slender shoulder, and Dianne and I quietly slink off to continue our mingling field trip, leaving Klaus to face his past, his former love who has arrived with her future.

Another attractive man wiggles his finger to invite me over to his group.

Whoa, I think, *me?*

He is from South America, humorous and an enjoyable conversationalist. Others mill around, joining in from time to time. *Hey*, I think, *these people are friendly and fun. I can do this. I'm capable of having conversations with strangers.* My second glass of that sparkly, pink, bubbly rosé has given me liquid courage!

It turns out to be a really fun evening, but it grows late and I suddenly feel thoroughly exhausted. Inspired by this precursor to the season of jolliness, I wave farewell to this friendly and generous group of revelers and head back out toward the cement underbelly of the parking garage.

The storm is in full force now, and my crummy old umbrella turns inside out when the wind hits it. *Oh well*, I think, *no need to try and look good anymore; I'm going home.*

I find the correct elevator—a large shiny chrome door—and as I push the button, I notice a pigeon lying in the debris of the grate in front of the elevator door. Its head is not at a natural angle; the neck is twisted down into the slot of the slippery grate. My first instinct is to pick it up, try to see if it's just stunned from hitting the massive door, which, with its mirrored surface, must have tricked the bird into thinking it was flying toward a companion.

Is it breathing, or is that the blustery wind striking its feathers? I stand frozen and getting soaked, struggling with leaving this creature to die alone. Is it possible to twist its little head back on? Can I save this bird, bring it back to life, watch it fly off into the dark? I stare down at it, unable to move.

Unlike the small creature knocked from its nest beside the Madison River, there is no mother who will save this bird. And there is no hummingbird feeder for me to fill with nourishment so that it can survive. This bird is dead . . . I can't fix dead.

The rain batters against the metal of the elevator door, reflecting a drenched woman, long past middle age, out on her own. What am I doing?

I never thought I'd have to do this again. My ambivalence about moving on to new relationships infects me like the onset of a bad flu.

We think we'll grow old with the person we've chosen, but our plans for how life will go can shatter in an instant—just like the delicate neck of a pigeon making its way through a stormy night who mistakes a shiny reflection of itself for a companion.

CHAPTER 25

When the root is deep, there is no
reason to fear the wind.
—Chinese proverb

On this last night of Día de los Muertos 2018, I carefully dissemble the altar, preserving its pieces for another year. I take down the pictures of those whose spirits have once again been released back into the unknown country where they dwell. The veil between the world of the living and the dead has closed, and those of us still here are left behind as the dead fly away into an ethereal landscape of our imagining. We can't know where they wander; we only know the dull ache of forever missing them.

Tenderly, I place the images of their smiles—the posed instants of their lives, captured and long frozen in black and white and color—into a file where they will reside, stacked one upon the other, until another year passes and the woven threads between worlds become transparent again. With a sick feeling in the pit of my stomach, I wonder if there will be new faces on the altar next year. Will anyone carry on the tradition and someday place me with them?

Unable to stay with these thoughts, I continue to take the altar down. Tasks are always helpful in moments of dread.

I return feathers, bones, and mementos once precious to my dead to the places where they will hibernate until next year. I return the fishing gear to the garage, turning on the light that reveals a chaos I cannot seem to manage no matter how many times I clear it. It's like sorrow: you think you have a handle on it, and then it comes crashing into your chest without notice, announcing itself as a gale-force wind that rages just beneath the surface of your organized, supposedly sane world.

Out of reach, above my head, are old crawdad traps, and I see John with Ben years ago on the pier at Lake Tahoe, pulling up buckets of those wriggling, disgusting creatures, Ben screaming in delight and then, true to the commitment to catch-and-release, lowering them back into the cold blue waters.

The worn wooden 1940s rafters of the garage, bastions of disorganization, contain boxes of long-forgotten treasures, old Christmas-tree stands piled on top of one another in the hopes that the next Christmas they will be remembered and be allowed to do their job once again, and containers of memories. They are beyond my reach—I don't have the strength to pull down objects to inspect. Is it all meaningless junk to be cleared? The wings of the bright yellow model airplanes—battered replicas of flight built by John long before I knew him, grounded on the eves of the old garage—are broken, but I somehow cannot imagine breaking the planes themselves into bits and tossing them into the trash.

How do you throw away a life?

In cupboards blocked from access by boxes not yet recycled and a table too heavy for me to lift on my own are the remains of objects—pictures, a lovely set of china that was always brought out for Christmas—I inherited from my parents and their parents. I cannot bear to toss my father's college diploma, earned when he was only twenty years old. Broke and finding his way during the Great Depression, he bussed tables in the university cafeteria to the sniggers from his fellow, more well-off students. A dusty and pungently moldy picture album featuring my young and beautiful mother as a high school student is buried among photos of people, long dead, whose names I will never know. I cannot bring myself to carry these remembrances of those once alive to a fetid graveyard in some garbage dump.

Another winter approaches, and the shadows gathering in the darkening skies of this last night of Día de los Muertos remind me of the shadows of the ferocious storms in Montana, how those dark clouds obscured the sun until the explosion from the sun's corona hitting the earth shot particles of light through our atmosphere and created the northern lights on that July day a year and half ago when I scattered John's ashes.

We whirl around in a dizzying dance from darkness to light and then light to darkness and back again; our lives explode, but we are carried along regardless of our limited ideas and plans. The shadows of the departed continue to haunt our dreams. Grief has no finish line, no real conclusions. We get dealt a hand we didn't want and have to play it anyway—you gotta play it as it lies. And in the end, you do just that, even when you don't feel like it (maybe especially when you don't feel like it), because it's the right thing to do.

And so, my story remains unfinished.

And it is not an exceptional story. I'm not special. I am not famous. I am just a woman living the same grieving story that has been lived by humans throughout time, because loss is the inevitable price we pay for being alive. And the more deeply we connect with others, the heavier the loss is to carry. You change, your grief changes, your life changes, and still you continue. The exhaustion of sadness becomes a part of your flesh and, over time, turns into scar tissue that will remain a part of you forever.

From the early-hour horror of John's heart rupturing—the moment when the ground I had known was torn away by a terrible wind and I was blown into a timeless, watery world—to the banks of the Madison River, where I nearly sank into the drenched earth along with John's ashes, to the mice-killing fields in my garage to the clink of glasses of bubbly rosé with strangers with whom, for a moment, I found community, I've had to find my way. And somehow, through the storms, the raging winds, and the torrential rain that swept through me like an uncontrollable tempest, the roots deep within my being held. These roots that are wound around my heart and set in the deep ground of my being did not break, even as I was carried by a monstrous, crying wind into unrecognizable realms that left me breathless and weary to my bones. Our roots, when deep, hold us through the ravages of grief, through the darkness of winter, and through the losses that will eventually come and take us away from all that we have known and loved.

Still, loss takes us to the outermost realms of our souls. I recall the story of a mother whale giving birth only to have her calf die within an hour of its birth. The scientists following this exceptional occurrence by boat noted that the grieving mother carried her calf the sixty to seventy miles she swam each day, pushing it up from the depths with her nose, all the while fighting strong currents and likely not eating. She continued to do this for days after its death. In their report, the scientists stated, in their measured, statistical manner, that it seemed as though she was not quite ready to give up her child. They wrote of the physical exhaustion of keeping her offspring with her, bringing it back up from the depths each time its dead weight carried it to the bottom of the sea. Could they not understand the emotional toll she experienced while struggling on, swimming without ceasing, keeping her calf from sinking away from her, taken by the currents into its burial ground in the depths?

Finally, she was forced at last to surface and swim away . . . alone.

I turn off the light by the fireplace mantle that has been home to the dead for the last few days. I imagine myself like the mother whale, swimming north to join her pod on their annual return to the Pacific Northwest—the place where I was born. I struggle against a current within me to remain with the memories of my life with John, to reside in the shadows of the past. But I cannot place myself with the dead; my roots are here, with the living. I am not yet among the departed.

I extinguish the Día de los Muertos candle and leave the darkened room, ready to join the living. My world is with them. I bend down to touch the roots beneath me, and I am grateful.

EPILOGUE: THE RETURN OF MIS

She was like the sun;
she knew her place in the world.
She would shine on again regardless
of all the storms and changeable weather.
—Nikki Rowe

Encrusted with the burnt sienna mud of tears and blood, Mis slithers down to the waters of an epic river. Covering the skin of her body are the slippery scales of a trout; they shimmer in the hues of a rainbow. The brown-and-gold-feathered wings of her arms are flung open as if to capture the gusts of wind that blow about her, gathering the air into the struggling madness of the wild animal clawing at the walls of her heart.

She comes alone. She has no guide to light her way in the ebony darkness she carries. There is no minstrel to sing her back to life with ballads of love. She has wailed alone three long years while the apple tree in the backyard has leafed out and born fruit season after season. The lemon tree her lover fought to preserve through years of drought has survived and is now heavy with bittersweet lemons that will never touch his lips.

Far from home, she crawls on all fours, her hands like the paws of a great, hairy wolf, over rocks slippery with moss to reach her lover's dead body. Reaching the bank beside the rush of stormy water, however, she finds only ashes, pieces of bone. She brings the chalky remains to her muzzle and devours what remains as if she could hold him within her forever.

A wildness surges through her, and her heart is torn open as the wind grows ferocious. The seawall within her breaks, a watery world floods forth, and the past three years of her life erupt across the jagged, broken edges of her heart, memories shattering and shredding on the earth beneath her, piercing her heart like torn branches.

She becomes a hummingbird screaming from a cob-webbed, neglected feeder at a grieving woman to nourish it. She is an urban pigeon with a shattered neck reflected in a chic and shining elevator door. She is a tiny song sparrow flung to the ground from its nest next to a raging river during a storm.

The guttural screaming of a woman reaches her through a monstrous wind, and the incoherent sounds spewed by the faces surrounding her, their mouths open, become words that swirl around her—"I'm sorry, I'm sorry." He is dead. A uniformed young man stays by her and then disappears in the first hours of a horrific dawn, never to return.

An exploding sun sending psychedelic hues across Big Sky Montana bursts into flames and becomes the dark urban skies over the home where she lives alone.

Tiny gray bodies of dead mice rain down.

Old clothes fly out of unused closets; unworn shoes tossed in unmatched piles are thrown about in the blustery gale. An unknown man starts a job in a suit he has received, donated by an unseen and nameless man who no longer has use for earthly goods.

She floats in a battered boat with a young fishing guide who wears a tattered, beloved hat on a mighty river.

The electricity of the storm illuminates an upscale chrome-and-glass cocktail lounge in a faraway and fashionable city. A fine rosé wine is sipped from elegant stemmed glasses; nervous laughter and silent sighs are heard across celestial spheres.

Images of the dead on all the altars of Día de los Muertos transform into a collage of a past that was. They reveal in black and white and color the many lives we live in our one lifetime. Candles will be lit for more dead as the years go by in an inevitable and yet somehow timeless passing. A future that will never happen becomes the future of all that will occur in its place.

She sees the face of a son abandoned as he enters the world as a young man, left fatherless for the remaining days of his life. She blesses the man he is becoming.

Scattering and blowing apart in the torrential tempest that surrounds her, she passes through a timeless portal and loses herself in a watery world. Minutes, hours, days, and years become an endless circle. A minute will pass and become a lifetime . . .

The future she will never know with her lover flies off into a lightening sky as the feathers of her outstretched wings become arms and the wind blows the feathers high into a robin's-egg blue sky. Her claws fall off; her hands emerge beneath the fur of the wolf paws. Her scales peel off and slip into the river and metamorphose into a trout the color of a rainbow, who swims off into chill waters. One day, this same creature will be caught by a fly fisherman and released back into another wild eddy in a faraway river.

She leaves scattered feathers, bits of slippery scales, and parts of herself by that river. An imprint of her soul will remain in a small park nestled between mighty purple mountains, and the mark left by her soul is as real and rugged as the small bone fragments and gray ash she leaves there. She is stripped naked, exposing the worn creases of her aging skin. Evanescent creature, she is saying goodbye to a life that is over; she can no longer wait for what will never be, for who will never return. Transformed in an acceptance of aloneness, she departs for an unknowable future.

She will come for you in your darkness. She will wrap wings that have become arms about your grief and hold you in the losses of your life. She will carry you over rivers and mountains through storms. Listen for her. She will master a harmony of comfort and courage and sing its songs to herself. She will teach them to you. And from your keening will emerge a song you will sing out as you travel through a grief you believed unbearable. And you will fall, you will fall, you will fall. And you will rise ... again and again and again.

ACKNOWLEDGMENTS

First, thank you to Brendan Bassi of the El Cerrito Police Department, who did not leave me alone but stayed with me during the first few hours after John's death. I still have his card on my refrigerator.

Sometimes angels fall to earth to shepherd us through storms and hold us up until we can stand on our own again. With gratitude to Chris Armstrong; Lou Dangles; Sandra Bryson; Wilma Friesema; Cathy and Dale Thorne; Cathi and Tony Christo; Steve Lipson; Richard Heasley; Michael O'Neill; Dianne Shumay; Jim Fishman; Alexis, Ted, and Dominic Mazzoli; Leslie Weir; Bruce, Jake, and Clara Lengacher; and Michelle Redell.

In memory of Diane Gravenites.

Thank you to Bill and Shash Woods for our time on rivers and for giving me the story of Mis.

I am grateful to Peg Miskin for putting John's ticket in the Casting for Recovery raffle and for giving me the opportunity to take the trip to Montana in his place, and to Jeanne and Ed Williams for offering Rainbow Valley Lodge in Ennis, Montana.

And a shout-out to "Dirty" Mike Elliott for guiding me to catch the biggest fish of my life.

With appreciation to Wayne Eng—you may yet again see me on the river.

Thanks to Krissa Lagos and Barrett Briske of She Writes Press, who have helped clean up the mess of all my books. Thanks also to Shannon Green for her steadfast attention to keeping me on track!

With gratitude to Caitlin Hamilton Summie of Caitlin Hamilton Marketing and Publicity, LLC, for her determination, encouragement, and generous soul.

And a deep and loving bow to Brooke Warner, who has been my steadfast partner in the writing of this book, holding not only my story but also *me* in her compassionate hands. She is a true companion of my heart on this odyssey.

I dedicate this story with love and gratitude to Ben Leonard, for giving me so much joy. Even though this is a recurring joke, Danny, you know it's true!

ABOUT THE AUTHOR

Cheryl Krauter is an existential humanistic psychother-apist with more than forty years of experience in the field of depth psychology and human consciousness. Her background in theater arts, working with performing artists, visual artists, and creative people, has inspired her work. After her cancer diagnosis in 2007, she began to focus on people who have been diagnosed with cancer and other life-threatening illnesses, as well as their partners, family members, and caregivers. Her two published books, *Surviving the Storm: A Workbook for Telling Your Cancer Story* (Oxford University Press 2017) and *Psychosocial Care of Cancer Survivors: A Clinician's Guide and Workbook for Providing Wholehearted Care* (Oxford University Press 2018), grew out of this work.

Author photo © Nan Phelps

SELECTED TITLES FROM SHE WRITES PRESS

She Writes Press is an independent publishing company founded to serve women writers everywhere. Visit us at www.shewritespress.com.

Naked Mountain: A Memoir by Marcia Mabee. $16.95, 978-1-63152-097-6. A compelling memoir of one woman's journey of natural world discovery, tragedy, and the enduring bonds of marriage, set against the backdrop of a stunning mountaintop in rural Virginia.

Splitting the Difference: A Heart-Shaped Memoir by Tré Miller-Rodríguez. $19.95, 978-1-938314-20-9. When 34-year-old Tré Miller-Rodríguez's husband dies suddenly from a heart attack, her grief sends her on an unexpected journey that culminates in a reunion with the biological daughter she gave up at 18.

Rethinking Possible: A Memoir of Resilience by Rebecca Faye Smith Galli. $16.95, 978-1-63152-220-8. After her brother's devastatingly young death tears her world apart, Becky Galli embarks upon a quest to recreate the sense of family she's lost—and learns about healing and the transformational power of love over loss along the way.

The First Signs of April: A Memoir by Mary-Elizabeth Briscoe. $16.95, 978-1631522987. Briscoe explores the destructive patterns of unresolved grief and the importance of connection for true healing to occur in this inspirational memoir, which weaves through time to explore grief reactions to two very different losses: suicide and cancer.

Filling Her Shoes: Memoir of an Inherited Family by Betsy Graziani Fasbinder. $16.95, 978-1-63152-198-0. A "sweet-bitter" story of how, with tenderness as their guide, a family formed in the wake of loss and learned that joy and grief can be entwined cohabitants in our lives.

Patchwork: A Memoir of Love and Loss by Mary Jo Doig. $16.95, 978-1-63152-449-3. Part mystery and part inspirational memoir, *Patchwork* chronicles the riveting healing journey of one woman who, following the death of a relative, has a flashback that opens a dark passageway back to her childhood and the horrific secrets that have long been buried deep inside her psyche.